AF073815

Midweek Recipes
Jess Elliott Dennison

April 2024

Hello and welcome to the first of (what will hopefully become!) a new series of books that I'm independently publishing from Elliott's Studio: my green-walled space that sits on a quiet residential street in the southside of Edinburgh. Since renovating the former Sciennes Road newsagents back in 2020, I've dedicated my Studio to recipe development, seasonal cookery demonstrations, visiting food writers and the makers and artists that inspire my food the most.

I'm starting this exciting (and slightly daunting) independent publishing venture with *Midweek Recipes* as I have a feeling that the simple meals I cook for my little family – week in, week out – is where I might be of most use to you in the kitchen. I've filled this book with easy, comforting favourites like my juicy tomato sugo with fennel seed and white wine (page 41) for tossing through your favourite pasta along with a mountain of grated Parmesan. We eat this tomato pasta every week in our house. It's cheap, on the table in 15 minutes (exactly the length of the 2 *Hey Duggee* episodes needed to keep our toddler Nora distracted!), and as tasty as you'll find in Italy. There's also my pillowy yoghurt flatbreads with different topping ideas to see you though the seasons (page 56). Thanks to my hack of adding miso paste to a very basic dough of natural yoghurt and plain flour, they taste like you go to the effort of keeping your own sourdough starter (which I can't seem to ever keep alive), and are a versatile base for dunking into the curry and soup recipes elsewhere in this book.

Rarely a week goes by in our house without Philip or I making a batch of crispy-edged, molten Cheddar and kimchi fritters (page 95), a quick round of lemony sage-fried eggs on toast (page 28), a pan of white beans cooked in wine with crispy breadcrumbs (page 84), or some sort of minestrone-style soup in an attempt to clear out the bottom of the fridge and get some vegetables into Nora (page 111). I've included guidance for making all of these most-rotated dishes from our house in this book.

Although I don't have a particularly sweet tooth, I find sometimes I just need that little midweek pick-me-up or extra bit of comfort, especially in the colder months. We live in an old cottage in the Scottish Borders so hot pudding on December evenings is as necessary as a woolly jumper. Towards the back pages you'll find my school dinner-inspired self-saucing chocolate sponge (page 141). It's by no means the fanciest dessert in my repertoire, but oh, how it really hits the spot when you need a bit of nostalgic comfort and only have store-cupboard basics to hand. Also in the puddings chapter you'll find a really custardy clafoutis using Earl Grey-soaked prunes that takes on the flavour of a fluted French canelé and doubles as a special breakfast the next morning (page 153). There's also my marmalade-toast sponge (page 143) – drown it in cream then flop straight onto the sofa; and a treacle fig tea loaf that I'm desperate for you to try with a chunk of your favourite cheese (page 151).

Reflecting on more than 12 years of working in food, which has included running my own restaurant for 5 of those years, writing 3 previous books, hosting seasonal cookery demonstrations, and testing and styling hundreds of other writers' recipes; I've realised there are a few common themes that run through all of my cooking. So as you flick through, expect to find lots of acidity, usually in the form of fresh lemon juice or a really good vinegar for balancing any richer flavours I've included. (Side note: great-quality vinegar is such an underrated ingredient. I look out for any unusual bottles made by natural winemakers. They make a really useful gift, and tend to be packaged beautifully). I use herbs, both woody and soft, in abundance year-round, so you'll be seeing lots of those. Quick-pickled shallots or onions, chilli flakes and fennel seeds are somewhat of an addiction at this stage, so you'll spot those throughout, too. I'm hoping the main thing you notice as you flick through is that I've written this book with accessibility of ingredients, ease of preparation, and simplicity in mind. From these pages I want you to feel covered for fresh, uplifting cooking, Monday through to Friday. Hopefully with flavours and textures so good that you'll want to eat from it on the weekend with mates over, too. Fingers crossed, anyway!

Perhaps it goes without saying, but for me, it's absolutely vital that a printed recipe simply *works*, no matter the level of confidence or experience of the home cook following it. So for the past few months, as I've been writing, these recipes have been sent out to a bank of 165 recipe testers who have very kindly blind-tested the dishes without a photo or introduction for reference. Thank you recipe testers, I owe you big time for your invaluable feedback and insight on this body of work.

Although I'm no photographer, it felt really important that I took all the photos myself in this book on my dodgy old camera as a way of highlighting how straightforward and personal these recipes are. Equally important to me was that this book was printed locally, or in the UK at least. I'm therefore delighted that this book has been printed by a small family business in Wales. I've been fortunate to work with Glasgow-based designer Maeve Redmond who understood my vision for the layout from the get-go, so thank you, Maeve. My former colleague Gemma Hinstridge, who was a delight to work with on so many projects back at Jamie Oliver, has been very patient with all of the copy-editing on this book. My assistant Phoebe Moon has been golden as usual, helping me to cook and photograph all of the recipes on a ridiculously tight (self-inflicted!) deadline. Lilly Hedley's illustrations and lino-cuts bring extra cheer to the pages.

My poor husband Philip has been quizzed and probed for feedback at every mealtime for the last few months, so thank you for being so supportive, Philip. I hope you can enjoy your dinner in peace now. Finally, I can't not mention Mum and Dad for their ongoing cheerleading in the creation of *Midweek Recipes*, on all things Elliott's, and for allowing me to turn my old bedroom into some sort of book fulfilment centre. I promise I'll allow you to retire properly and relax soon!

Reader, working to bring *Midweek Recipes* together these past few months with the talented gang I just mentioned has been such a joy, and I really hope these pages bring equal use, optimism and deliciousness to your kitchens,

Jess

Go-To Ingredients

I'm often asked which ingredients I use most in my cooking and there's nothing I love more than nosing round my friends' kitchens to see what they stock up on, too. Our kitchen at home is tiny, so as much as I aspire to have a walk-in pantry filled with every imaginable ingredient, the reality is I have to keep supplies pretty limited and hard-working.

I find that if you've got great staples like delicious olive oil, sea salt and lemons on the workbench; a few good quality tins and jars, beans and packets of pasta in the cupboard; some fresh herbs, maybe a jar of capers or gherkins and some Dijon mustard in the fridge; then everyday cooking can be really simple yet really interesting. Plus, with the ever-increasing price of food, this streamlined approach keeps things affordable for us.

Oils — I always have 3 types of oil to hand: Cold-pressed Scottish rapeseed oil for its optimistic colour (see the aioli on page 19) and gentle, delicious flavour. I use extra-virgin olive oil for drizzling over salads, soups and pastas, and am happy to pay a bit more for something special. I also keep a cheap, neutral vegetable oil for frying fritters (page 95), schnitzel (page 133) and breaded fish (page 135).

Sea Salt — This is a non-negotiable in my cooking. I always use flaky sea salt such as Maldon, Halen Môn or Blackthorn rather than mechanically produced fine table salt as it's completely natural and brings out the flavours of your other ingredients. I encourage you to season your food at the start of the cooking process, for example, when frying onions or vegetables to draw out moisture and season from the get-go.

Citrus and Vinegar — So often I think it's a touch of acid that elevates home cooking to restaurant standards. You'll spot lemons in many of the recipes in this book, including their zest as much as their juice. Deep-flavoured vinegars such as aged cider vinegar or rosé vinegar are such an underrated ingredient for lifting everyday ingredients, too. If you've got jars of capers or pickles sitting in the fridge you can use their brine to lift your dishes as well, just bear in mind that they'll be salty already.

Dairy — I always buy salted butter and full-fat milk, cream and crème fraîche as to me, they simply taste better than the reduced-fat versions.

Eggs, Meat and Fish — I go for large free-range eggs, but don't worry if you're making a recipe with smaller-sized eggs – it's not going to cause you any issues. We cook predominantly vegetarian throughout the week, so when I do buy meat and fish from my local fishmonger and butcher, I know it's higher welfare and more sustainably sourced. I've written these recipes with cheaper cuts in mind, for example, crisping up sausage meat to get it really sticky and caramelised then cooking in milk as per the meatballs on page 125.

Jars of Marinated Artichokes, Mustard, Capers, Gherkins, Pickles, Olives — our fridge is filled with jars of salty, briny things that I use to add brightness and acidity to our mealtimes. You'll notice I often stir some of these through yoghurt to make a fresh sort of tartare sauce – ideal with the fish baps on page 135 – or to create a punchy dressing, as in the tuna, potatoes and green beans recipe on page 123.

Fennel Seeds and Chilli Flakes — I don't use that much black pepper in my cooking, but I do have an addiction to crushed fennel seeds and chilli flakes, which I suppose are my replacement for the heat and perfume that peppercorns bring. They bring great base flavour to my tomato pasta on page 41, quick beans on page 84 and fridge-raid soup on page 111. Look out for the big bags of spices in the Asian section of a larger supermarket as they're far better value than the tiny glass jars.

Panko Breadcrumbs, Sushi Rice and Kimchi — In addition to soy sauce, miso paste, rice wine vinegar and sesame oil, I find it's worth a trip to the Asian supermarket every now and again to get these three extra ingredients. I like to quickly fry panko breadcrumbs with olive oil and lemon so I've got a crispy topping for the beans on page 84. They also make the schnitzels on page 133 and fish baps recipe on page 135 a doddle to fry. Once you've mastered perfectly cooked, perfectly seasoned sushi rice there's no turning back, so I urge you to try the recipe on page 103. Korean kimchi from the Asian supermarket in a large jar has way more depth of flavour and texture than the tiny little jars you find in British supermarkets, and is far better value. My favourite kimchi brand is Chongga.

White Wine — Wine is such a brilliant shortcut to add complexity, depth and acidity to soups, braises and stews, as seen in the beans on page 84, for example. Don't worry about using anything special, but of course, the more interesting the wine, the more interesting the flavour you're going to get in your finished dish. I occasionally use red wine in winter cooking, but I love how white wine keeps day-to-day cooking light and bright.

Tins and Jars of Beans, Pulses and Lentils — Tinned beans and lentils can really speed up midweek cooking. I use cheap tinned chickpeas to make a delicious creamy mash to serve with sausage meatballs on page 125, and in the sour tomato curry on page 67. Where beans are the hero, I'll use a jar of Bold Bean Co. or Brindisa beans, such as in the recipe on page 84. The extra quality is worth every extra penny. If I'm being organised, I'll cook a bag of dried lentils to make the dish on page 87, for example, but a ready-cooked sachet or tin is great too.

My Style of Cooking and Eating

There are sauces such as rapeseed aioli and a roughly chopped salsa verde; sides like quick-pickled onions, good cucumbers and green salad; plus finishing touches like crisping herbs and capers that crop up in my cooking year-round. This way of eating with layers of texture, colour and acidity is what makes my food feel like mine, so if you've been to my cookery demonstrations at my Studio before then the chances are you'll be familiar with some of the techniques below. If not, I really urge you to try integrating these extra tasty little bits and bobs into your daily cooking.

A Really Good Green Salad

Growing up, Mum would *always* make a lemony green salad to go along with whatever the main dish for dinner was. It was often my job to make the dressing and I still use the same little red plastic juicer that she bought from British Home Stores in the 1980s for squeezing lemons in my Studio today. I urge you to buy whole lettuce rather than those bags of pre-cut and often overpriced leaves that tend to just wilt the minute you open the bag. Butterhead lettuce, cos, baby gem and frisée are my favourites. They only need a quick wash and dry then some fresh lemon juice or your favourite vinegar, a pinch of sea salt and some of your best olive oil. Toss through the leaves then tweak to your liking. Of course, Dijon mustard, capers, shavings of hard cheese and fresh herbs always make a delightful addition to salads – I particularly love adding tarragon and flat-leaf parsley leaves to mine. Also – don't be scared to just tear lettuce leaves from their stem to keep them large, bouncy and beautiful when piled up on a plate. I'll only ever finely shred lettuce when stuffing it into a burger bun!

Marinated Tomatoes For Eating all Summer Long

If you ever ate at my restaurant in the warmer months when it was still open, then I imagine you ate some version of my marinated tomatoes. The key is to get hold of great quality, ripe, in-season tomatoes. I get mine from my friend Margaret who grows them at Bemersyde Estate near our house in the Scottish Borders or from the Isle of Wight company. Often, I'll just buy the finer, on-the-vine ranges from the supermarket for eating at home. The key for delicious tomatoes is keeping them out of the fridge, ideally near a window and some sunshine. Sit your tomatoes in a paper bag for a day or two if they need a little help ripening.

I roughly slice my tomatoes in drunk, wonky slices then dress them in good vinegar, sea salt, a whole clove of peeled garlic, a pinch of chilli flakes, fennel seeds and my best oil. They'll happily sit in this juicy concoction for up to a day so they're ideal for taking to gatherings, for spooning over toast or eating with a roast chicken. Any leftover tomatoes and marinating juices can be blended into a really fresh pasta sauce served at room temperature, just remember to fish out the garlic clove.

Fried Herbs and Capers

So much of the enjoyment in eating is about all five senses, so I'll often fry woody herbs or even a spoonful of capers to add inviting textures to a dish. In the summer, it's oregano from our garden that I'll fry to go on very simple tomatoes on toast (see page 27), or crisped-up rosemary to elevate a chicken schnitzel (page 133).

Quick-Pickled Onions and Herbs

You may notice that I very lightly pickle onions and shallots in lots of the dishes throughout this book. I love how they provide freshness and crunch and they're brilliant for cutting through richer ingredients like the fried halloumi on page 60, pastry on page 77 and the Pau Bhaji on page 69. Once you get into the swing of doing quick onion pickles with whatever herbs are in the fridge you'll become addicted like me, I'm sure of it.

A Punchy Side Yoghurt

Quite often I quickly whip up different side yoghurts to bring interest and contrast to the main dish: tartare sauce for the fish baps on page 135, for example; minted yoghurt to go with halloumi wraps on page 60; and cucumber yoghurt to lighten the rich toasted almond curry on page 73. I always keep two types of yoghurt in our fridge: natural yoghurt for making the wraps on page 56 and to have with seasonal fruit and muesli; plus a thicker Greek-style yoguhrt to turn into these types of side dips.

Artichoke, Olive and Lentil Tapenade

The delightful combination of artichokes and Kalamata olives fried with fennel seeds, chilli, lemon peel, rosemary and lentils started life as a pasta sauce in my first cookbook back in 2018. I've later discovered that if you blend the same ingredients into a tapenade, it makes for the most incredible crostini topping, or serve it with hummus, flatbreads and crudité. The lentils provide a sweet, creamy backnote to the strong flavours of the olives and spices. Try a spoonful of the tapenade on toast with eggs (see page 37), or served on the Tuscan-style soup (page 111).

Makes a small bowl / 10 spoonfuls

1½ tbsp olive oil
2 fat garlic cloves, peeled, crushed and roughly chopped
¼ tsp chilli flakes
¼ tsp fennel seeds
¼ lemon, skin peeled with a speed peeler
1 stem rosemary, leaves stripped, stem discarded
90g Kalamata olives, pitted and drained
75g jarred artichokes in oil, drained
½ tsp brown sugar
100g cooked green lentils (tinned or from a sachet)

Heat the olive oil in a frying pan on a high heat then add the garlic, chilli flakes, fennel seeds, lemon peel, rosemary, olives, artichokes and brown sugar. Fry on a high heat for 2–3 minutes, then add the lentils and ½ tsp lemon juice. Cook out for a further minute on high then, using a hand blender, blitz until you have a chunky paste.

NOTES
+ Keep in the fridge for up to 5 days in a sealed container.
+ You can use any variety of pitted olives.

Scottish Rapeseed Aioli

If you cut me open then this stuff would be running through my veins! You can use a neutral vegetable oil or olive oil to make your aioli, but I use cold-pressed rapeseed oil as it gives the most incredible yellow that brightens any plate.

Makes a small bowl / 8 spoonfuls
Takes 10 minutes

1 free-range egg yolk
1½ tsp Dijon mustard
¼ tsp sea salt flakes
½ garlic clove, peeled and finely minced
    (I use a microplane for this)
100ml cold-pressed rapeseed oil
    (in a jug for easy pouring)
zest of ¼ lemon
1½ tsp lemon juice

Place the egg yolk, Dijon mustard, salt and garlic in a mixing bowl, then stir with a whisk to combine. Drop by drop, pour in the oil while continuously whisking until very thick and wobbly. This should take a couple of minutes and don't be tempted to rush pouring in the oil or your aioli coud split. Stir in the lemon zest and juice which will loosen it slightly, then have a taste for seasoning.

NOTES
+ If you place the bowl on a few sheets of damp paper, it will stop the bowl moving about as you whisk.
+ If you have any soft herbs in the fridge that need using up, finely chop them and add to the aioli. Tarragon, parsley and basil all work brilliantly.
+ It keeps for up to 5 days in the fridge.

Carrot Rappé

If you ever get a fixed-price lunch menu in Paris, then this is often the starter. I adore how punchy and simple this carrot dish is, and all you need is a box grater. It doesn't get much better than a grilled steak or some sausages with these carrots and some crusty baguette for eating out in the garden on a sunny afternoon.

Serves 2 as a small side
Takes 5 minutes

¾ tsp Dijon mustard
1 tsp lemon juice
½ tsp cold-pressed rapeseed oil or olive oil
pinch sea salt flakes
1 large carrot (120g)
1 tbsp parsley, finely chopped
1 tarragon sprig, leaves picked, stalk discarded

Stir the mustard, lemon juice, oil and salt together in a small bowl. Peel and grate the carrot on the large side of a box grater then – very importantly – squeeze away as much of the carrot juice in your hands over the sink as possible before adding to the dressing. Stir in the parsley and tarragon, then eat straight away.

NOTES
+ Try this with the chicken schnitzel on page 133.
+ If you're making this ahead on a larger scale, keep the grated carrot in a colander, and the dressing in a small bowl, then combine just before serving so that the dressing doesn't become diluted with carrot juice. You want the carrots to feel really fresh.

Salsa Verde

I urge you to chop your salsa verde with a sharp knife on a board rather than blending it in a food processor as you'll get a beautiful texture with each spoonful offering a different mouthfeel and pop of flavour.

Makes a small bowl / 8 spoonfuls
Takes 5 minutes

1 small bunch parsley (15g), leaves only
1 small bunch basil (15g), leaves only
1 small bunch mint (15g), leaves only
1 garlic clove, peeled
1½ tbsp capers
(30g anchovies in olive oil, optional)
1 tsp Dijon mustard
2 tbsp cider vinegar, white or red wine vinegar
120ml your best extra-virgin olive oil
    or cold-pressed rapeseed oil

Finely chop the herbs, garlic, capers (and anchovies, if using) together on a board then place in a small bowl. Stir in the mustard, vinegar and olive oil.

NOTES
+ Covered with cling film or in a jar, salsa verde will keep in the fridge for 3-4 days. It will lose some of the vibrancy of the green, but will be just as delicious.
+ If eating from the fridge, allow your salsa verde to return to room temperature before serving.

Really Good Cucumbers

These cucumbers have all the flavours of 'bread and butter pickles', but are fresher and crunchier.

Serves 2
Takes 5 minutes

½ shallot or ¼ white onion (15g)
½ tbsp capers
zest of ¼ lemon and 2 tsp lemon juice
2 tsp cold-pressed rapeseed oil or olive oil
tiny pinch fennel seeds
tiny pinch chilli flakes
tiny pinch caster sugar
pinch sea salt flakes
100g cucumber
1 tbsp torn dill fronds or a few tarragon leaves

Peel and finely slice the shallot, then add it to a bowl along with the capers, lemon zest and juice, rapeseed oil, fennel seeds, chilli flakes, sugar, and salt. Slice the cucumber into thin rounds then stir through the dressing. Throw in the herbs then serve up straight away.

NOTES
+ A 100g chunk of regular cucumber is fine for this, but baby cucumbers are extra crunchy and flavourful. They're increasingly available in the larger supermarkets. Or look for a Lebanese cucumber at the greengrocer.
+ Try these with the kimchi fritters on page 95.

Good things on toast

Tomatoes on Toast
with crispy capers, oregano
(and anchovies, if they're your thing)
27

Sage-Fried Eggs on Toast
with lemony greens
28

Dill-Scrambled Eggs on Toast
with lemon and feta
30

Soft-Boiled Eggs and
Chilli Burnt Butter on Toast
with yoghurt and dill
33

Artichoke, Olive and Lentil Tapenade Toast
37

Tomatoes on Toast with crispy capers and oregano

Tomatoes on Toast
with crispy capers, oregano
(and anchovies, if they're your thing)

This is what I eat for lunch throughout the summer when the tomatoes are at their best. If you can get your hands on great tomatoes, I beg that you keep them out of the fridge as they'll have so much more flavour when they've been kept at room temperature.

Serves 2
Takes 10 minutes

2 slices white sourdough bread
2 large, ripe tomatoes, (at room temperature)
sea salt flakes
(pinch chilli flakes, optional)
1 tbsp good olive oil, plus extra to drizzle
2 stems oregano, leaves stripped, stalks discarded
2 tbsp capers
1 garlic clove, peeled
(6 anchovies in oil, optional)

Toast your bread until golden and crunchy. Meanwhile, slice up the tomatoes then generously sprinkle with sea salt (and chilli flakes, if using).

Heat the olive oil in a small frying pan on a medium heat, then throw in the oregano and capers. Fry for 2-3 minutes until crispy. Take care, as the caper brine tends to spit at you as it hits the hot pan.

Meanwhile, rub the toast with the garlic clove. Layer up the tomatoes, crispy oregano and capers; plus extra oil (and anchovies if you like, too).

NOTES
+ You'll find a quick recipe reel for this on my instagram.
+ Substitute the oregano for any herbs you have to hand.

Sage-Fried Eggs on Toast
with lemony greens

For these eggs, I am forever grateful. They're what I became known for in the early Elliott's Cafe days, and responsible for us having queues down the street on weekend mornings! It's all about simplicity and texture: the crunch of the toasted crust, the spongier bit of inner bread that has soaked up all the lemony juices, the crispy, frilly edges of the fried egg and those silky, oozy yolks.

Serves 2
Takes 10 minutes

3 tbsp cold-pressed rapeseed or olive oil,
   plus another 2 tbsp
1 handful sage leaves (approx 10g)
2 free-range eggs (or 4 eggs if you're really hungry)
sea salt flakes
2 slices good bread
2 handfuls spinach (approx 60g)
1 lemon: ½ for juicing, ½ for zesting
(pinch chilli flakes, optional)

First, heat 3 tbsp oil in a non-stick frying pan, throw in your sage and allow it to crisp up before tossing to one side of the pan. Crack in your eggs then, using a spatula or fish slice, flick the crispy-sage over the top of the eggs. Fry on high for 3–4 minutes until the edges are super crisp and the yolks are still a little runny (or cook to your liking). Season with plenty of salt, then remove from the heat.
   Toast your bread until golden and crunchy.
   In a second pan, heat the additional 2 tbsp oil, plus the spinach, lemon juice and a pinch of salt. Fry on high for 1 minute, or until just wilted. Pile up the spinach onto the toast then top with the fried eggs and plenty of lemon zest – I find a microplane is most helpful for this. (Sprinkle over the chilli flakes if using.)

Sage-Fried Eggs on Toast with lemony greens

NOTES

+ You can substitute the spinach for any leafy greens: kale, cavolo nero, even wilted watercress, rocket or baby gem lettuce all work well.
+ If you have a gas hob, you can char the toast on an open flame for a minute or so for an extra layer of flavour.
+ Rubbing the toast with a peeled garlic clove before piling up with the wilted spinach is a delicious move – just not too early in the morning!

Dill-Scrambled Eggs on Toast
with lemon and feta

Back when I had the Cafe, I would write the day's menu up on the blackboard with chalk. Thanks to my awful handwriting, we would often get an order for these "dull scrambled eggs" which would make me giggle. These are far from dull, however! Just a few simple ingredients make this familiar quick-fix supper something really special.

Serves 2
Takes 5 minutes

2 slices sourdough bread
3 tbsp cold-pressed rapeseed or olive oil
1 large handful dill (approx 15g)
4 free-range eggs
sea salt flakes
50g feta cheese
1 small lemon

Toast your bread until golden and crunchy. Place the oil in a large frying pan on a high heat. Tear in the dill and allow it to fry for 1 minute until fragrant. Crack the eggs and a pinch of salt into the pan, reduce the heat to medium then, using a spatula, keep gently folding.

Crumble in the feta to allow it to start melting just before the eggs are fully cooked. Try not to over-whisk the eggs in the pan too much, as you would when making traditional scrambled eggs, as it's lovely to get some mouthfuls of yolk and little nuggets of melted feta.

Divide the cooked eggs between the toast. Use a microplane to zest over plenty of lemon zest, then serve each portion with a lemon wedge so that each person can squeeze over as much or as little juice as they like.

Dill-Scrambled Eggs on Toast with lemon and feta

Soft-Boiled Eggs and Chilli Burnt Butter on Toast with yoghurt and dill

Soft-Boiled Eggs and Chilli Burnt Butter on Toast
with yoghurt and dill

I love how the contrast between creamy yoghurt and chilli burnt butter transforms a humble boiled egg into a beautiful little meal. I've thrown on some dill here, but the more soft herbs the merrier. Basil, parsley, oregano are all very welcome.

Serves 2
Takes 15 minutes

4 large free-range eggs
2 slices sourdough bread
30g butter (salted or unsalted)
1 tsp paprika
¼ tsp chilli flakes
150g Greek yoghurt
sea salt flakes
1 small handful dill (approx 10g)
½ lemon

First, bring a pan of water to the boil, carefully place in the eggs, then gently simmer for 7 minutes. Drain, then crack the base of each egg before placing them in a small bowl of cold water for a few seconds – this will stop them cooking and give you 'jammy' middles. Peel away and discard the shells.

Meanwhile, toast the bread until golden and crunchy. Heat the butter in a small pan for 2–3 minutes until it's a dark, nutty brown colour. Remove from the heat then stir in the paprika and chilli flakes.

Spread the yoghurt over the toast, top with a tiny pinch of salt then lightly smash on the eggs with a fork and another pinch of salt. Pour over the paprika butter, tear over the dill, zest over some lemon, then finish with a squeeze of lemon juice.

Artichoke, Olive and Lentil Tapenade Toast

Artichoke, Olive and Lentil Tapenade Toast with soft boiled eggs

I often make my salty, creamy artichoke and olive tapenade to spread on crostini as a little welcome snack at events in my Studio; but add a few boiled eggs and a thick slice of toast and you're sorted for lunch or a light supper. This is particularly good with a glass of chilled wine.

Serves 2
Takes 15 minutes

4 large free-range eggs
2 slices sourdough bread
a few spoonfuls of tapenade from page 18
sea salt flakes
½ lemon

First, bring a pan of water to the boil, carefully place in the eggs then gently simmer for 7 minutes. Drain, then crack the base of each egg before placing them in a small bowl of cold water for a few seconds – this will stop them cooking and give you 'jammy' middles. Peel away and discard the shells.

Meanwhile, toast the bread until golden and crunchy then spread with the tapenade. Smash over the peeled eggs and finish with plenty of salt and a squeeze of lemon.

Pasta

Tomato and Fennel Seed Rigatoni
41

Cavolo Nero and Parmesan Spaghetti
43

Lemon Cream Linguine
46

Broccoli, Parmesan and Lemon Orecchiette
48

Triple-Cheese Orecchiette
51

Tomato and Fennel Seed Rigatoni

Tomato and Fennel Seed Rigatoni

We eat this in our house every week as it's Nora's favourite. I like to use tins of whole plum tomatoes as they make the sauce really fresh and juicy, but chopped tomatoes are fine if that's what's already in the cupboard. Please don't skimp on the generous amount of oil I've suggested, it's going to give you a silky sauce that tastes like it's been simmering on the stove for hours and won't feel 'oily' as such, I promise.

Serves 2
Takes 15 minutes

200g rigatoni, penne, spaghetti,
   or your favourite dried pasta
3½ tbsp olive oil or cold-pressed rapeseed oil
2 fat garlic cloves
¼ tsp chilli flakes
1 tsp fennel seeds
1 × 400g tin plum tomatoes
150ml white wine
½ tsp sea salt flakes
¼ tsp caster sugar
35g Parmesan cheese

First, bring a full kettle of water to the boil, then cook the pasta in a medium pan on a high heat in the boiling water for 8–10 minutes, or until 'al dente'. (I don't bother salting the pasta water for this recipe.) Stir occasionally to prevent the pasta from sticking, and drain in a colander once ready (you don't need to reserve any cooking water).

   Meanwhile, add the oil to a large frying pan on a medium heat. Peel and finely crush the garlic (or finely grate on a microplane), then add to the pan along with the chilli flakes and fennel seeds. Gently fry for 1–2 minutes until the garlic is just on the edge of turning golden, ensuring it doesn't burn. Throw in the tomatoes, crush with a fork or wooden spoon, then pour the wine into the empty tin to wash out any tomato juices and add it to the pan along with the salt and sugar. Crank up the heat so it reduces into a glossy sauce while the pasta is cooking. Taste a few times to check for seasoning.

Finely grate the Parmesan cheese (don't bother washing away any raw garlic juices on the grater as they'll be delicious), then throw most of the cheese into the sauce, along with the drained pasta. Stir until the pasta is really well coated. Your sauce shouldn't be too soupy or too concentrated, but silky and glossy. Divide between 2 bowls and top with the remaining Parmesan.

NOTES
+ Throwing olives, capers and/or jarred artichokes into this sauce at the end of cooking is always a good idea.
+ You can of course substitute the white wine for red wine, but I like the zesty lightness that white wine brings. Your wine doesn't need to be anything fancy. Dry cider works well too.
+ We love rigatoni for this, but use whichever pasta shape you have to hand.
+ If you enjoy the flavours in this sauce but fancy swapping the pasta for some more nutritionally-dense beans, then try the recipe on page 84.

Cavolo Nero and Parmesan Spaghetti

This *River Cafe* classic has become a regular fixture in my kitchen as I just love knowing how much cavolo nero I'm getting into my little family without them realising. The vibrant green sauce is just as divine when tossed through great quality jarred butter beans or queen chickpeas, gnocchi, or on the side with a steak or piece of grilled fish. A great sauce to have up your sleeve.

Serves 2
Takes 15 minutes

3 fat garlic cloves
150g cavolo nero
200g dried spaghetti
1¼ tsp sea salt flakes
40g Parmesan cheese
2 tbsp cold-pressed rapeseed or olive oil
(40g ricotta, optional)
½ lemon
a drizzle of your best olive oil

First, bring a full kettle of water to the boil. Peel the garlic, strip the leaves from the cavolo nero (discarding the tough stems); then cook the spaghetti, cavolo nero and garlic in a medium pan of boiling water with 1 tsp salt on a high heat for 5 minutes. Using tongs, carefully remove the cavolo nero and garlic and transfer to a large, deep bowl. Continue cooking the pasta until 'al dente' (probably another 3–5 minutes). Stir occasionally to prevent the pasta from sticking, then drain in a colander making sure to reserve a mugful of the starchy cooking water.

Finely grate the Parmesan then add to the bowl of cooked kale and garlic. Add in the oil and ¼ tsp salt then, using a hand blender, blitz until you have a smooth sauce. Spoon the sauce back into the pan, along with the drained spaghetti. (It doesn't need to be on the heat as it will still be warm.) Toss to nicely coat the spaghetti with the sauce until silky – adding a few splashes of reserved water if you think it needs it. Taste for seasoning, then divide between 2 bowls. (If using the ricotta, crumble over the top.)

Then, using a microplane, finely zest over the lemon. Cut the lemon into wedges so each person can squeeze over fresh lemon if they wish. Finish with an extra drizzle of your best oil.

NOTES

+ I'll often make a variation on this spaghetti, using orecchiette pasta and a handful of cooked chickpeas from a jar as I love how they sit in the 'little ears' along with a pool of the beautiful green sauce. If you're looking for a break from gluten, the sauce on good quality jarred beans alone is divine.
+ This cavolo nero sauce sits very happily in the fridge for a couple of days: just keep it in an airtight jar or container to hold on to the vibrant green colour.

Cavolo Nero and Parmesan Spaghetti

Lemon Cream Linguine

If I was only allowed to pick one of the pastas from this book then this would be the one. The marriage of lemon, garlic and cream makes this linguine feel so chic. It's easy yet elegant, and a reminder that less is so often more when it comes to cooking. Sometimes I want loads of different colours and textures for dinner, and sometimes I just want this pale, citrusy beauty.

Definitely one to make for your loved ones.

> *Serves 2*
> *Takes 15 minutes*
>
> 1 tsp salt
> 200g dried linguine or spaghetti
> 2 garlic cloves, peeled
> 1 lemon, zested, plus 1½ tbsp juice
> 30g Parmesan cheese
> 30g butter
> 60ml double cream

First, add the salt to a medium pan of water then bring to the boil. Cook the pasta until 'al dente' or to your liking, this usually takes between 7–9 minutes. Use a mug to reserve a few spoonfuls of the cooking water. Drain the pasta in a colander.

    Meanwhile, get organised with the remaining ingredients so that you can bring the sauce together really quickly once the pasta has cooked. Using a microplane, finely grate the garlic, zest the whole lemon and finely grate the Parmesan. Measure out the lemon juice, butter and cream.

    Heat the butter in a large frying pan on a medium heat then add the garlic and lemon zest, gently frying for 1–2 minutes until fragrant, but not catching or burning. Reduce the heat to low then add in the Parmesan and

Lemon Cream Linguine

cream until melted into a glossy, creamy sauce. Remove from the heat.

Toss in the pasta, stir a few times to encourage your sauce to become beautifully silky, then add the lemon juice, stirring constantly. Add in a few splashes of reserved cooking water if you think the sauce needs loosening slightly then taste for seasoning. Divide between 2 bowls then tuck right in.

NOTES

+ If you have any leftover double cream, I strongly recommend making the fool on page 163 – you can use whichever berries you have in the freezer.

Broccoli, Parmesan and Lemon Orecchiette

Most of the time I prepare broccoli so that it's only just cooked, and therefore tender with plenty of vibrancy. This is the opposite approach where you want the broccoli to become mushy and creamy, almost pesto-like, for folding through your favourite pasta. I adore how much comfort this green bowl of pasta brings and I imagine that, like me, you'll almost always have most of these ingredients in your cupboards.

Serves 2
Takes 30 minutes

1½ tsp sea salt flakes
1 broccoli (approx 350g)
3 stems rosemary
4 tbsp extra virgin olive oil, plus extra to finish
5 fat garlic cloves
200g dried orecchiette
½ lemon
25g Parmesan cheese
(pinch chilli flakes, optional)
extra virgin olive oil, to taste

Bring a large pan of water and 1 tsp salt to the boil. Chop up the broccoli into really small pieces, including the stalk (discarding the really tough part at the end of the stem).

Boil the broccoli for 5–10 minutes or until really soft. Scoop out with a slotted spoon, and scoop out a mug of the cooking water, too. Top up the pan with boiling water from a kettle – you'll use this pot of water to cook your pasta shortly.

Meanwhile, strip and roughly chop the rosemary, then add, along with the oil, to a large frying pan on a medium heat. Cook for 1–2 minutes until crispy while you peel and roughly slice the garlic. (I know it looks like a lot of oil, but please trust me that the finished

Broccoli, Parmesan and Lemon Orecchiette

pasta won't be oily.) Reduce the heat to low then add the garlic, fry for 1–2 minutes until fragrant, then transfer the cooked broccoli to the garlicky pan along with ½ tsp salt. Add ½ mug of the cooking water, then increase the heat to high, stirring regularly for 8–10 minutes until you have a creamy, mushy sauce. You can use a fork or potato masher to encourage the broccoli to break down, and you can top up with a little more cooking water if you need to at any point.

Cook your pasta in the water you used to cook the broccoli until 'al dente', this usually takes 8–9 minutes, then drain in a colander.

Meanwhile, using a microplane, finely zest the lemon into the mushy broccoli, then squeeze in the juice, discarding any pips. Grate the Parmesan, then add to the sauce too, along with a pinch of chilli flakes, if you like. Stir your cooked pasta through the broccoli sauce, have a final taste for seasoning, then serve up with plenty of lovely olive oil over the top.

NOTES

+ Orecchiette is my favourite pasta shape for this sauce, but farfalle, rigatoni or any short shape will work perfectly – just use whatever pasta you already have in the cupboard.
+ If anchovies are your thing, 4 or 5 fillets fried off with the garlic at the beginning of the sauce makes for a delicious addition.
+ When chopping the broccoli, I like to nip off the leaves and cook them whole as they look beautiful when plating up.

Triple-Cheese Orecchiette

I make this at the Christmas markets that I host in the Studio every year to keep everyone cosy as they do their shopping. Who doesn't love the sight of a tray of bubbling cheesy pasta coming out of the oven? It's a seriously hearty supper, so it works brilliantly with greens dressed in a mustardy vinaigrette to balance out the richness of the cheese.

Serves 4
(or 2, with the best leftover lunch for the next day)
Takes 1 hour

400g dried orecchiette or macaroni
1 tsp plus ½ tsp sea salt flakes
3 fat garlic cloves, peeled
35g salted butter
3½ tbsp plain flour
150ml white wine
300ml whole milk
35g Comté cheese
25g Parmesan cheese, plus 5g for the top
50g Cheddar cheese
1 tsp Dijon mustard
¼ tsp miso paste

First, preheat the oven to 200°C (400°F/gas 6).

Cook the pasta in a pan of boiling water with 1 tsp salt on a high heat for 8–9 minutes, or until cooked through, then drain in a colander.

Meanwhile, use a microplane to finely grate the garlic into a frying pan. Add the butter then fry the garlic on a high heat for 2 minutes, or until golden but not burning. Stir in the flour and cook out for a further 2 minutes on high, stirring regularly. Pour in the wine, a few splashes at a time, stirring regularly until you get a thick paste. Reduce the heat to medium then add in the milk, 50ml

Triple-Cheese Orecchiette

at a time. Keep stirring until you've got a lump-free, creamy sauce. Remove from the heat.

Grate all the cheeses on the large side of a box grater, then stir into the sauce until melted along with the mustard and miso paste. Stir in the pasta, transfer to a baking dish (mine is 24 × 17cm), finely grate the remaining Parmesan over the top then bake for 20 minutes or until golden and bubbling.

NOTES

+ The shallot green beans from page 123 or the green salad on page 15 make the perfect side to cut through the richness of this pasta.
+ This pasta freezes brilliantly, so you could double the recipe, cook one straight away then stash one in the freezer for a lazy evening.

Flatbreads

Yoghurt and Miso Flatbread Dough
56

Courgette, Oregano and Crème Fraîche Flatbreads
59

Halloumi, Cucumber and Olive Flatbreads
60

Lamb, Cumin and Tomato Flatbreads
62

Yoghurt and Miso Flatbread Dough

I use the combination of miso paste and natural yoghurt to hack the fermented flavour of sourdough in these incredibly versatile, fluffy flatbreads. It's worth buying a jar of miso for making these alone as they're excellent for mopping up the curries in this book, or simply for topping with one of the ideas in this chapter.

Any colour or type of miso will do, and if you don't have any to hand, just use a pinch of sea salt instead. I've listed plain flour below but quite often I'll do half plain flour, half wholemeal too.

Makes 2 large flatbreads
Takes 15 minutes

125g plain flour, plus extra for rolling out
½ tsp baking powder
½ tbsp miso paste
100g natural yoghurt

Stir the flour, baking powder, miso paste and yoghurt together in a large bowl. (Don't worry about adding any salt to the dough as the miso is enough to season it).

Dust your work surface with plenty of flour then knead the dough for a couple of minutes until smooth.

Halve the dough then, using your hands or a rolling pin, roll out into 2 flatbreads roughly 12 cm in diameter.

When you're ready to cook, heat a large non-stick frying pan (ideally cast iron) to the highest heat (you don't need to add any oil to the pan). Lay a flatbread in the pan and cook for 2 minutes without interfering. Carefully, using tongs or a fish slice, flip and cook for a further 2 minutes, or until charred at the edges and puffing up in the middle. Repeat for the second flatbread. You may need to reduce the heat to medium once you're on to the second one.

Yoghurt and Miso Flatbread Dough

NOTES

+ You can make the dough ahead and leave it covered tightly with cling film, to rest for up to 24 hours out of the fridge. If I'm being really organised, I'll make the dough in the morning before heading to work, or I'll call ahead to Philip to make up the dough when I'm leaving work. But it works just as well if you use the dough immediately.

Courgette, Oregano and Crème Fraîche Flatbreads

Courgette, Oregano and Crème Fraîche Flatbreads

Make these in the summer when courgettes are most tender and at their best. Just don't hold back when frying the courgettes: a really high heat will give you the most incredible sweet, fragrant juices that soak into the flatbread.

Makes 2 flatbreads
Takes 15 minutes

2 tbsp olive oil or cold-pressed rapeseed oil
2 courgettes, finely sliced into wonky rounds
sea salt flakes
2 fat garlic cloves, peeled
tiny pinch chilli flakes
½ lemon
2 flatbreads from page 56
2 tbsp crème fraîche
2 tbsp aioli from page 19
1 handful fresh oregano, basil or parsley leaves
    (approx 10g)

Heat the oil in a large frying pan over a high heat. Add the courgettes and a pinch of salt then hard-fry for 8 minutes until charred at the edges and soft in the middle. Stir regularly. Reduce the heat to low and finely grate in the garlic (I use a microplane for this) then gently sweat for 2 minutes until fragrant. Remove from the heat.

Add the chilli flakes and the lemon's zest then have a taste, tweak the seasoning and spiciness to your liking.

Top the flatbreads with the courgettes, pan juices, a dollop of crème fraîche, aioli and fresh herbs of your choice. Cut the lemon into small wedges and squeeze over the juice.

Halloumi, Cucumber and Olive Flatbreads

Is there anything more crowd-pleasing than hot fried halloumi rolled into a pillowy flatbread with a fresh little crunchy salad and loads of herby yoghurt? These are very popular in our household!

Makes 2 flatbreads

225g pack halloumi cheese, drained
1½ tbsp olive oil or cold-pressed rapeseed oil
   (or oil from a jar of sun-dried tomatoes),
   plus a drizzle
10 green or black olives, drained and pitted
1 ripe tomato
2 jalapeños (from a jar in brine)
2 flatbreads from page 56
(chilli sauce, optional)

CUCUMBER SALAD
½ onion
6cm piece cucumber
1 tbsp cider or white wine vinegar
pinch fennel seeds
1 small handful dill, roughly chopped (approx 10g)

MINT YOGHURT
½ garlic clove, peeled
150g Greek or natural yoghurt
½ tsp dried mint

Pat the halloumi dry with a piece of kitchen paper, then cut into slices. Heat the oil in a frying pan, then fry the halloumi on a medium-high heat for 2–3 minutes on each side until golden. Remove from the heat then add the olives to the pan to gently warm them through.

To make the cucumber salad, finely slice the onion and cucumber then add to a bowl with the vinegar, fennel

Halloumi, Cucumber and Olive Flatbreads

seeds and dill. In a separate bowl, finely grate in the garlic (I use a microplane for this), then stir in the yoghurt and dried mint. Slice up the tomato and jalapeños.

To serve, spoon the yoghurt over the flatbreads, then pile up the halloumi, olives, cucumber salad, tomato and jalapeños. Add an extra drizzle of olive oil if you like, plus chilli sauce if you want it extra spicy.

NOTES
+ If you do have spare oil from a jar of sun-dried tomatoes, add a final drizzle to your wrap before tucking in as it'll be extra delicious.
+ A pinch of sumac and some chopped parsley are also very welcome here.

Lamb, Cumin and Tomato Flatbreads

I reckon this lamb mince flatbread is the most-cooked recipe from my *Tin Can Magic* book, so I couldn't not include it in this book with the added guidance of making your own flatbreads. Use beef if you prefer, but I love how the fattiness of the lamb combines with the spices to make a really juicy, fragrant topping.

Makes 2 flatbreads
15 minutes

2 tsp cumin seeds
1 tsp fennel seeds
1 tbsp cold-pressed rapeseed oil or olive oil
250g minced lamb
1 tsp sea salt flakes
½ tsp ground cinnamon
½ tsp chilli flakes
1 × 400g tin plum or chopped tomatoes
2 flatbreads from page 56

MINT AND CUCUMBER YOGHURT
½ cucumber, deseeded and finely diced
1 tsp dried mint
pinch sea salt flakes
1 small garlic clove, peeled and finely grated
5 heaped tbsp Greek yoghurt

TO SERVE
1 handful mint leaves (approx 5g)
pinch sumac
½ lemon

First, add the cumin seeds and fennel seeds to a large frying pan over a high heat then dry-fry for 1–2 minutes until fragrant. Transfer to a pestle and mortar or chopping board to roughly crush. Return the pan to

Lamb, Cumin and Tomato Flatbreads

a high heat, then add the oil and the lamb; fry for 3–4 minutes until crispy and gaining some nice dark colour.

Stir in the crushed spices, salt, cinnamon and chilli flakes until fragrant. Pour in the tomatoes, then simmer on high for 10 minutes, stirring occasionally until reduced and sticky.

Stir together the cucumber, mint, salt, garlic and yoghurt in a small bowl. Spoon the mince over a flatbread, then add a dollop of the yoghurt. Tear over the mint, add the pinch of sumac, then zest over the lemon to finish.

Cara Guthrie Ceramics

9x gold jugs

07577 608 109
hello@caraguthrieceramics.com
web | caraguthrieceramics.com
instagram | caraguthrieceramics

Cara Guthrie Ceramics

12x colander (ten)

07577 608 109
hello@caraguthrieceramics.com
web | caraguthrieceramics.com
instagram | caraguthrieceramics

Cara Guthrie Ceramics

10x gold colanders

07577 608 109
hello@caraguthrieceramics.com
web | caraguthrieceramics.com
instagram | caraguthrieceramics

Cara Guthrie Ceramics

9x ten jugs

07577 608 109
hello@caraguthrieceramics.com
web | caraguthrieceramics.com
instagram | caraguthrieceramics

Cara Guthrie Ceramics

3x ten jugs
3x gold jugs
20x gold bowls

07577 608 109
hello@caraguthrieceramics.com
web | caraguthrieceramics.com
instagram | caraguthrieceramics

Cara Guthrie Ceramics

3x ten colanders
5x gold colanders
5x gold bowls

07577 608 109
hello@caraguthrieceramics.com
web | caraguthrieceramics.com
instagram | caraguthrieceramics

ELLIOTT'S

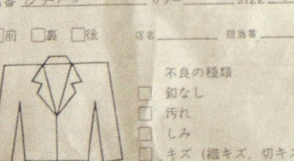

555

不良品カード　6月2日

ブランド＿＿＿
品番 0418 056　カラー＿＿　SIZE F

□前　□裏　□後　店名＿＿＿　担当者＿＿＿

不良の種類
□ 釦なし
□ 汚れ
□ しみ
□ キズ（織キズ、切キズ）
□ ほつれ
□ しわ
□ 縫製不良
□ 色ちがい
□ その他（説明のこと）

不良個所に○印をつけること

踊えて不良

Anglobal
ゆみ

Curry and curry pie

Sour Tomato, Mustard Seed
and Chickpea Curry
67

Pau Bhaji
with hot-buttered rolls and onion
69

Toasted Almond Chicken Korma
73

Fennel, Pea and Coriander Pie
with raita and apple, tomato & cucumber salad
77

Sour Tomato, Mustard Seed and Chickpea Curry

Sour Tomato, Mustard Seed and Chickpea Curry

I lean into the slightly sour quality of tomatoes in this curry by stirring in a splash of vinegar towards the end of the cooking process. It makes for a bright, interesting contrast to richer, creamier curries; including the Toasted Almond Chicken Curry on page 73.

Serves 2 generously, with leftovers
Takes 35 minutes

1 white onion, peeled and finely sliced
2 tsp yellow mustard seeds
2 tbsp vegetable or cold-pressed rapeseed oil, plus a splash
pinch sea salt flakes, plus more to taste
5 green cardamom pods
5 fat garlic cloves
1 tsp tomato purée
1 tsp garam masala
1½ tsp ground cumin
pinch ground turmeric
pinch chilli flakes
6 ripe tomatoes (approx 600g)
1 × 400ml tin full-fat coconut milk
1 tsp caster sugar
1 × 400g tin chickpeas, drained (I use the tin lid to drain to save on washing up)
1 tbsp malt vinegar or cider vinegar, plus more to taste
(25g butter, optional)

First, fry the onion and mustard seeds in the oil and salt on a medium heat for 8 mins in a medium pan, stirring occasionally. Crush the skin of the cardamom pods, then throw the whole pods into the pan with the onion. Peel and roughly crush the garlic cloves with the side of your knife, then roughly chop, add to the pan, and fry for a further 5 minutes, ensuring to stir regularly so that the garlic doesn't burn. You may want to add a tiny splash of more oil to the pan.

Stir in the tomato purée and allow it to a cook out for a minute or so, then stir in the garam masala, ground cumin, turmeric and chilli flakes. Roughly chop the tomatoes then add to the pan along with the coconut milk, caster sugar, chickpeas and vinegar. Allow the curry simmer for 10–15 minutes until slightly reduced. Taste for seasoning before serving – you may want to add more salt, chilli or vinegar. If you like, you can finish by melting in some butter, this will make your curry sauce extra silky and glossy.

NOTES

+ Simply-cooked basmati rice is excellent with this curry, or make the flatbreads on page 56.
+ If you have any leftovers, water it down slightly, then crack eggs into it like you would a shakshuka and enjoy for breakfast the next day – so good!

Pau Bhaji
with hot-buttered rolls and onion

I can't visit Dishoom without ordering this dish, so this is my simplified version of the recipe from their incredible cookbook (one to add to your collection if you don't already own it!). I'm told that if you order Pau Bhaji in Mumbai then it comes topped with a huge slab of butter. So this is my message to not scrimp on the butter front.

Serves 2, with plenty of leftovers
Takes 35 minutes

2 carrots
2 parsnips
1 small sweet potato or regular potato
2 large florets cauliflower or broccoli
1 small handful green beans
2 white onions
3 tbsp cold-pressed rapeseed or vegetable oil
sea salt flakes
3 garlic cloves
¼ tsp ground turmeric
2 tsp garam masala
2½ tsp ground cumin
1 handful frozen peas (approx 85g)
1 × 400g tin plum tomatoes
½ lemon
2 × white bread rolls/morning rolls
lots of butter for spreading

First, boil the kettle.

Chop the carrots, parsnips, potato, cauliflower and green beans into small dice (don't worry about them being neat dice as you're going to blend them later anyway). Add to a pan, cover with boiling water, then simmer for 12 minutes, or until very soft. Drain in a colander.

Meanwhile, finely slice 1½ onions (save half an onion for garnish later), then fry with the oil and a pinch of salt on a high heat for 5–6 minutes to get things going, stirring regularly. Peel and roughly chop the garlic, then reduce the heat to low and stir it into the onions along with the turmeric, garam masala and cumin. Fry for 3–4 minutes until fragrant, ensuring the garlic doesn't burn.

Throw the drained vegetables into the onion pan along with the peas, the tin of tomatoes and a splash of water. (I slosh the water around the tomato tin to help get all the contents out.) Simmer for 5 minutes then, using a hand blender, blitz most of the mixture, leaving behind a few whole peas and chunks of vegetable. You're looking for a warm, thick, hummus-like texture. Check for seasoning – you might want to add more chilli – and you'll probably find it needs quite a bit of salt.

Finely dice the remaining onion half, then pop it into a small bowl and squeeze over the lemon's juice, discarding any pips.

Cut open the rolls, then lightly toast them by sitting them on top of the toaster or, carefully using tongs, over a gas flame. Spread them with a very generous amount of butter!

Divide the vegetable mixture between 2 bowls. Spoon over the lemony-onion topping then tuck in by scooping up with the buttery toasted rolls.

NOTES

+ Keep it vegan: up until the butter, this dish is completely vegan, so a good one to have up your sleeve for vegan friends coming over.
+ Make it meaty: stir 200g fried minced beef, chicken or pork through the Pau Bhaji mixture for a kheema-style curry.
+ If you have any fresh coriander or parsley in the fridge, this would be lovely torn over the top with the onion.
+ A fried egg on top always goes down well... although I find that's the case for most dishes!

Pau Bhaji with hot-buttered rolls and onion

Toasted Almond Chicken Korma

Toasted Almond Chicken Korma

Look, it's not often a cookbook encourages you to go out and order takeaway, but if you want to recreate what I would class as the best Friday night curry set-up then you're gonna have to go with me on this one.

Phone your local British-Indian curry house, order poppadoms, peshwari naans (very important!) and a couple of sides – some bhajis, rice, samosas and spicy okra, perhaps.

While you're waiting for your order, whip up this indulgent curry, the cucumber yoghurt from page 78 and some finely chopped coriander. The curry itself is incredibly rich, fragrant and layered with flavour thanks to the toasted almonds, spices and coconut milk.

Pull out your favourite condiments (Geeta's mango chutney, lime pickle and chilli sauce are a must for me), chill some beers, then thank me later.

P.S. The curry freezes perfectly, so it's worth making a huge batch.

Serves 2, with leftovers
Takes 30 minutes for chicken breast
/ 45 minutes for chicken thigh

75g ground almonds
2 white onions
1 tbsp cold-pressed rapeseed or vegetable oil
1½ tsp sea salt flakes
1 × 400g tin coconut milk (full fat)
2 good quality chicken breasts or 4 skinless, boneless chicken thighs
4 garlic cloves
4 cardamom pods
½ tbsp ground cumin
½ tbsp garam masala
½ tsp turmeric
pinch chilli flakes

pinch ground cinnamon
2 tsp brown sugar
thumb-sized piece ginger (15g)
zest of ¼ lemon
(1 tbsp sultanas or raisins, optional)

First, toast your ground almonds in a dry frying pan on a high heat for 2–3 minutes, or until lightly golden and smelling like freshly-made popcorn. Stir regularly, then transfer to a bowl so that they stop toasting and don't burn.

Peel and finely slice the onions then add to the pan with the oil, salt and a few spoonfuls of hard coconut fat from the top of the tin. Fry on a high heat for 7–8 minutes, stirring occasionally. It may feel unusual cooking your onions in the coconut milk, but you're looking for the edges to caramelise and slightly char.

Meanwhile, cut your chicken into large chunks then add to the pan and continue to fry on a high heat to seal the edges of the chicken for 2–3 minutes.

Peel, crush and roughly chop the garlic, then reduce the pan to a low heat and gently fry the garlic for 3–4 minutes until fragrant. Gently crush the cardamom pods with the side of your knife, then add them to the pan whole along with the cumin, garam masala, turmeric, chilli flakes, and cinnamon. Fry the spices for a minute or two then pour in the remaining coconut milk, half a tin of water, toasted almonds and the brown sugar.

Finely grate the ginger into the pan using a microplane (I don't bother peeling it). Discard any tough inner root that refuses to be grated. Simmer for 12–15 minutes, stirring regularly to bring that caramelisation off the bottom of the pan. If you're using chicken breasts, check that it's cooked through in the middle. If using thighs, you'll need to simmer for another 6–8 minutes.

Using a microplane, zest in the lemon peel just before serving. I also like to throw in some sultanas.

Toasted Almond Chicken Korma

NOTES
+ You could make the raita from page 78 to go with this curry.
+ Any leftovers are divine thrown into a slightly charred wrap with mango chutney, yoghurt, loads of fresh salad, tomatoes and cucumber.

Fennel, Pea and Coriander Pie with raita and apple, tomato & cucumber salad

Fennel, Pea and Coriander Pie
with raita and apple, tomato & cucumber salad

Having pie for dinner midweek feels like such a treat, and this one is super quick and easy to throw together. The yoghurt raita and fresh salad cut through the richness of the puff pastry, so the whole meal feels like a good balance of comforting and indulgent yet also fresh, nutritious and light.

I would say this pie could serve 4, but in all honesty, we always return for seconds! Any leftovers that you do happen to have are particularly good for lunch the next day.

Serves 4, but we make it for 2 of us plus a toddler and always return for seconds and polish it off!
Takes 50 minutes

PIE
1 large fennel (230g)
1 white onion
3 tbsp cold-pressed rapeseed or olive oil
½ tsp sea salt flakes
4 garlic cloves
¼ tsp chilli flakes
1 tsp mustard seeds
2 tsp ground cumin
½ tsp fennel seeds
zest of ½ lemon
1 large handful coriander (approx 20g)
90g frozen peas
1 × all-butter puff pastry sheet (320g)
1 tbsp milk

RAITA
½ garlic clove, peeled and finely grated
tiny pinch sea salt flakes
pinch ground cumin
125g Greek yoghurt
½ tsp dried mint

APPLE, TOMATO AND CUCUMBER SALAD
1 tsp lemon juice
6 ripe cherry tomatoes/2 tomatoes (approx 70g),
    finely sliced
½ apple, finely sliced (approx 60g)
75g cucumber, finely sliced
pinch sea salt flakes
1 tbsp coriander, finely chopped
½ tbsp cold-pressed rapeseed or olive oil
(½ red or green chilli, finely sliced, optional)

First, preheat the oven to 200°C (400°F/gas 6).

Finely slice the fennel and ¾ of the onion. Heat the oil in a large frying pan on a high heat, then fry the fennel and onion with the salt for 3–4 minutes.

Meanwhile, peel, crush and roughly chop the garlic. Measure out the spices and zest the lemon. Add to the pan and fry for 2 minutes, stirring regularly to ensure the garlic and spices don't burn. Roughly chop the coriander, then throw into the pan along with the peas. Add 2 tsp lemon juice, and fry for a further minute to allow the peas to begin defrosting. Remove from the heat then have a taste for seasoning – you may want to up the chilli as I'm cooking with a toddler in mind.

Unroll the puff pastry (keeping its layer of baking paper underneath) onto a baking tray.

Imagine the sheet of pastry is like a book, then fill half of the sheet with the pea filling. Using a pastry brush, wash a 1½ cm border with milk then fold over the pastry, as if you're closing the book. Pinch the edges or crimp with a fork, then use a sharp knife to make some light scores in a criss-cross pattern. Brush the top with the remaining milk, create a little incision in the middle of the pie to allow any steam to escape, then bake for 25 minutes or until deep golden brown.

Whilst the pie is baking, make the raita by stirring all the ingredients together in a small bowl.

Finely slice the remaining ¼ onion, then add to a separate bowl along with the salad ingredients. Have a taste for seasoning – you may want to add more lemon juice as it needs to be punchy to cut through the buttery pastry.

Once baked, cut the pie into quarters and serve up with the raita and salad. Delicious.

NOTES

+ You can easily substitute the fennel and coriander for leeks, spring onions, spinach, wild garlic and any other soft herbs you already have sitting in the fridge. Dill would work very well in this pie.
+ If you want to get organised, you could prep the pie right up to the point of baking, then just bake when you're ready to eat. If you want to be really organised, you could even double the quantities, have one pie for dinner, then pop a second in the freezer for another day.

Beans and lentils

Bay Lentils, Burrata and Salsa Verde
83

Tomato and White Wine Beans
with crispy lemon breadcrumbs
84

Warm Dill Lentils
with cumin spinach and yoghurt
87

Braised Fennel, Tomato
and Courgette Butter Beans
89

Bay Lentils, Burrata, Salsa Verde

Bay Lentils, Burrata and Salsa Verde

This dish is embarrassingly easy to prepare, yet feels like something you'd order in a restaurant as it's an assembly of such great ingredients. Some crusty baguette for mopping up the salsa verde and burrata juices is the only extra that might be needed, although a side of grilled sausages and a bottle of wine wouldn't go amiss either! You can definitely use pre-cooked lentils from a tin or sachet, from a brand like Merchant Gourmet, to make things ever easier too.

Serves 2
Takes 20 minutes

100g dried green or puy lentils
5 bay leaves
1 small onion, cut into quarters, don't bother peeling it
½ tsp sea salt flakes
2 tsp cider vinegar or red wine vinegar
tiny pinch chilli flakes
a few spoonfuls of salsa verde from page 21
1 burrata (150g drained weight), ideally kept out the fridge for a few minutes

First, place the lentils, bay and onion quarters in a small pan. Cover with cold water, bring to a boil then gently simmer for 15-20 minutes, or until the lentils are tender, or cooked to your liking. Drain well in a colander then discard the bay and onion.

Whilst still warm, toss the drained lentils in a bowl with the salt, vinegar, chilli flakes and a few spoonfuls of the salsa verde. Taste, then adjust the seasoning to your liking. Divide between two plates then tear over the burrata and spoon over some extra salsa verde.

Tomato and White Wine Beans
with crispy lemon breadcrumbs

This is essentially a poshed-up version of cheesy beans on toast. Personally, I think there's real beauty in delicious, beige comfort food (especially in Scotland's colder months). Fold through some torn kale leaves in the last few minutes of cooking the beans, or make the punchy green salad (on page 15) if you're looking for a bit of added greenery, though.

Also, the breadcrumbs are great over loads of other dishes, too: think soups, stews and pastas (including the broccoli orecchiette on page 48).

Serves 2
Takes 15 minutes

2 tbsp cold-pressed rapeseed or good olive oil, plus extra to finish
3 garlic cloves
½ tsp fennel seeds
¼ tsp chilli flakes
2 tbsp tomato purée
1 × 700g jar haricot or cannellini beans (I like Bold Bean Co and Brindisa) or 2 × good quality 400g tins
100ml whole milk
75ml white wine
½ tsp caster sugar
(2 bay leaves, optional)
30g Parmesan cheese
sea salt flakes

BREADCRUMBS
2 tbsp good olive oil
30g panko breadcrumbs
sea salt flakes
½ lemon for zesting

Tomato and White Wine Beans with crispy lemon breadcrumbs

Gently heat the oil in a frying pan over a low heat then peel and finely grate the garlic into the pan (I use a microplane for this). Add the fennel seeds and chilli flakes and fry for 1 minute until fragrant, ensuring the garlic doesn't burn. Stir in the tomato purée, increase the heat to high to cook out the purée for 1 minute, stirring regularly.

Using the jar lid as a sieve, drain away most of the bean juice, then pour the beans into the pan, crushing the last few beans from the bottom of the jar with your hands (this is going to make the sauce lovely and creamy). Add the milk, wine, sugar (and bay, if using). Simmer for 8–10 minutes on high, stirring regularly until combined into a thick, silky sauce.

Meanwhile, finely grate the Parmesan with a microplane (don't bother washing away any garlic juices that are remaining on the grater as they'll be delicious).

In another pan, fry the oil, panko breadcrumbs and a good pinch of salt together on a high heat for 2–3 minutes until golden. Stir regularly and don't walk away as they can burn easily. Transfer to a plate to stop them cooking.

Remove the beans from the heat, discard the bay leaves and stir in the grated Parmesan. Have a taste for seasoning. I find different brands of jarred beans vary greatly in saltiness, so season to your liking. Divide between 2 bowls then sprinkle over the golden breadcrumbs, plenty of lemon zest and lots of your favourite olive oil.

NOTES

+ Herbs would of course be a lovely addition to these beans. If using woody herbs like rosemary, sage or oregano, finely chop them and fry along with the oil and breadcrumbs. For soft herbs like parsley, dill or tarragon, just roughly tear and garnish with them at the end so that they stay fresh and perky.
+ Fried-off bacon, pancetta or sausage meat would also make a brilliant topping for the beans. Or make them as a side to roast chicken.
+ You can make these with tinned beans, but as it's such a simple set of ingredients it'll be nowhere near as good as the jarred-bean version.
+ Jarred butter beans are a great swap if you can't get hold of the smaller white beans, you'll just need to increase the milk to 150ml.

Warm Dill Lentils
with cumin, spinach and yoghurt

Tinned lentils are such a store-cupboard hero for speeding up your cooking, and here they not only provide hearty substance but are also a great carrier for the cumin-spiced spinach and braised dill. I really enjoy these lentils as they are, but add some grilled sausages or white fish if you'd like a fuller meal.

Serves 4, (or 2, with a great lunchbox each the next day)
Takes 25 minutes

2 white onions
3 tbsp olive oil
¼ – ½ tsp sea salt flakes
2 garlic cloves, peeled and crushed
3 tsp ground cumin
200g baby leaf spinach
1 large bunch dill (approx 20g), roughly chopped
2 × 400g tins green lentils in water, rinsed
   and drained
1 lemon
3 tbsp natural yoghurt

First, peel and slice the onions into half-moons, as finely as you can. Place the oil in a large frying pan then cook the onion with ¼ tsp salt over a low heat for 8 minutes. Add the garlic and cumin and cook for a further 5–6 minutes until the onion is really soft and sweet.

Meanwhile, rinse the spinach under plenty of cold water and drain completely, squeezing out any excess moisture. Add the dill to the onion along with the drained lentils and spinach. Zest in the lemon and squeeze in the juice of half, then increase the heat to high. Cover with a lid and steam for 1 minute until the greens are wilted but still retain some shape.

Warm Dill Lentils with cumin, spinach and yoghurt

Check the seasoning: you may want to add more salt and lemon juice.

Divide the lentils between your plates then dollop over the yoghurt and serve.

Braised Fennel, Tomato and Courgette Butter Beans

This recipe started life as the main dish I taught at my Summer Series of cookery demonstrations in 2022 and I haven't stopped making it since. The butter beans are the star of the show here, so try and use great quality jarred ones if you can. They're more expensive than tinned beans, but so worth it for the texture and flavour. This dish really is a celebration of summer produce, so I hope you enjoy making it.

Serves 4, (or 2 for dinner, with a great lunchbox the next day each)
Takes 30 minutes

4 tbsp cold-pressed rapeseed or olive oil
1 fennel, finely sliced
   (reserve the green tops for garnish)
1 tsp sea salt
½ tsp fennel seeds
pinch chilli flakes
4 garlic cloves, peeled and crushed
1 courgette, finely sliced
4 ripe tomatoes, roughly chopped
250ml white wine
1 tsp dried oregano or 4 stems fresh oregano,
   leaves stripped, stems discarded
   (reserve a few for garnish)
1 × 700g jar of giant butter beans
   or 2 × 400g tins of butter beans
1 lemon
extra virgin olive oil and black pepper to serve

Heat the oil in a large pan on a medium heat, add the fennel and salt to the pan and gently fry for 10–15 minutes until golden but not too brown. Crush the fennel seeds in a pestle and mortar, then add to the pan along with the chilli flakes.

Add the garlic, stirring regularly to ensure it doesn't burn. Then increase the heat in the pan and add the courgette. Hard-fry on a high heat for 2–3 minutes to get some colour on the courgettes, then clamp a lid on your pan so that the courgettes sweat and cook in their own juices for 5 minutes.

Throw the tomatoes, wine and oregano into the pan, simmer for 5 minutes, then add the butter beans, including the jar/tin juices. Cook for a further 5–10 minutes, or until reduced and the courgettes and tomatoes are really tender. Using the side of a wooden spoon, crush a few of the butter beans to thicken the stew.

Using a microplane, zest in the lemon, then have a taste. You might want to add a pinch more salt, or even some of the lemon's juice, depending on how acidic your wine is.

Serve up with the reserved fennel fronds and oregano leaves, plus extra virgin olive oil and black pepper.

NOTES
+ These beans are delicious warm or at room temperature, so ideal for a packed lunch the next day. They keep well if you make them a few days ahead, just re-taste for seasoning before serving.
+ If you like, you can also blend any leftovers to make a delicious, velvety soup.

Braised Fennel, Tomato and Courgette Butter Beans

Kimchi fritters, rice & noodles

Kimchi, Cheddar and Onion Fritters
with honey and lemon
95

Peanut Butter Chilli Noodles
99

Broccoli, Tofu and Sesame Soba Noodles
101

Sweet-Soy Omelette, Sushi Rice
with quick pickles
103

Kimchi, Cheddar and Onion Fritters with honey and lemon

Kimchi, Cheddar and Onion Fritters
with honey and lemon

My favourite toastie is a cheese and kimchi toastie, so that's the inspiration for these quick fritters. Biting into a pool of molten cheese with the background tang of spicy kimchi really is something memorable, yet they're a doddle to whip up. Simply served with rice or stuffed into a soft baguette (bánh mì-style), this might just be my favourite recipe in this book.

Makes 8 fritters – serves 2
Takes 15 minutes

1 large free-range egg
½ tbsp soy sauce
2 tbsp water
100g flour, ideally gluten-free (I like Dove's), but plain flour is fine too
175g kimchi (ideally the weight is made up of the fermented cabbage rather than the brine)
½ white onion
35g Cheddar cheese
3 tbsp vegetable oil
2 tbsp runny honey
½ lemon

Begin by stirring the egg, soy sauce, water and flour into a thick batter in a large bowl. Roughly chop the kimchi, finely slice the onion and roughly chop the cheese into small, random chunks then stir into the batter to combine.

Heat 2 tbsp oil in a large frying pan on a high heat, then drop heaped tablespoons of batter into the pan to create 4 fritters (or however many fritters will comfortably fit in your pan). Fry for 2–3 minutes, then carefully flip each fritter and cook for a further 2–3 minutes. Transfer to a plate lined with kitchen paper.

Kimchi, Cheddar and Onion Fritters with honey and lemon

Reduce the heat under the pan as it'll be very hot by this point, then add another tablespoon of oil, and the remainder of the batter to create another 4 fritters. Again, fry for 2–3 minutes on each side.

Divide the fritters between 2 plates, drizzle over the honey, squeeze over the lemon then tuck in.

NOTES

+ If you fancied a larger meal, you could cook some rice and greens to have with the fritters. Steamed broccoli, sugar snaps and spinach can be dressed in ½ clove finely grated garlic mixed with 1½ tbsp soy sauce and ½ tbsp rice wine vinegar. Or shove the fritters in a baguette with some quick-pickled carrots and cucumber and spicy mayo for a sort of bánh mì situation. Delicious!
+ It may seem weird asking for gluten-free flour in the batter mixture, but the lack of gluten makes the fritters extra crispy – just use plain flour if that's all you have, they will still be fantastic.
+ Different brands and batches of kimchi will have different strengths of heat so if your kimchi is on the mild side, you could always add some chilli powder or chilli flakes to the batter.
+ You could grate the cheese on a box grater if you prefer, but I love the random pools of melted cheese you find in the fritters from small chunks of cheese.

Peanut Butter Chilli Noodles

Peanut Butter Chilli Noodles

This is my go-to lunch when working alone as it takes less than 10 minutes and is ridiculously delicious. Yes, lunch should probably include some sort of vegetable, but sometimes a simple bowl of noodles is just what's needed to hit the spot.

Serves 2
Takes 10 minutes

2 flat nests medium egg noodles (approx 190g)
1 garlic clove
2 spring onions
4 tbsp smooth peanut butter
3 tbsp soy sauce
2 tsp cider vinegar
½ – 1 tsp chilli flakes
4 tbsp cooking water

First, bring a pan of water to the boil then cook your noodles for 3–4 minutes. Carefully use a mug to reserve a few splashes of the cooking water.

Meanwhile, peel and mince the garlic (I use a microplane for this) and finely slice the spring onion.

Drain the noodles in a colander then return them to the pan, off the heat. Stir in the garlic, peanut butter, soy sauce, vinegar and chilli until the noodles are coated in a glossy sauce. You may need up to 4 tbsp reserved cooking water to loosen it.

Transfer the dressed noodles to a bowl, then top with the sliced spring onion and serve.

NOTES
+ If you have any leftover kimchi from making the fritters on page 95, top with kimchi instead of/as well as the spring onion.

Broccoli, Tofu and Sesame Soba Noodles

Broccoli, Tofu and Sesame Soba Noodles

Once a month or so, I make a dedicated trip to our local Asian supermarket to stock up on my favourite condiments, sauces and noodles. I always leave the shop with several packs of soba noodles as the chewy buckwheat strands work so beautifully in quick stir-fries such as this one. When it's in season, purple sprouting broccoli and tofu is my favourite combination with the toasted sesame seeds and sauce; but of course, just substitute with whatever veg you need to use up.

Serves 2
Takes 20 minutes

180g soba noodles
   (Akagi Joshu is my favourite brand)
3½ tbsp sesame oil
1 tbsp rice wine vinegar
200g purple sprouting broccoli
100g firm tofu (I like The TofOO Co. brand)
4 cloves garlic
2 spring onions
2 tbsp sesame seeds
1 tbsp brown sugar
1 tbsp soy sauce
1 tbsp sriracha chilli sauce

First, bring a pan of water to the boil. Cook the noodles for 3–4 minutes, then rinse under plenty of cold water and drain. Add the noodles to a large bowl then toss through 1 tbsp sesame oil and ½ tbsp rice wine vinegar.

    Meanwhile, prepare all your produce: trim any tough ends off the broccoli, then slice any really wide stems lengthways. Drain the tofu then cut into small cubes. Peel, crush and roughly chop the garlic. Finely slice the spring onions.

Heat a large frying pan on a high heat then add the sesame seeds, toast for 1–2 minutes, or until golden and fragrant. Transfer to a plate.

Add 2 tbsp sesame oil to the pan then fry the broccoli and tofu for 3–4 minutes – you're looking for the broccoli to be charred at the edges but retaining some bite and for the tofu to gain some colour. Transfer to the plate with the toasted sesame seeds.

Reduce the heat to low then add ½ tbsp sesame oil, followed by the garlic. Fry for 2 minutes, or until fragrant, ensuring it doesn't burn. Add the sugar, stir regularly for 30 seconds as it caramelises, then add in the soy, ½ tbsp rice wine vinegar and the sriracha.

Remove the pan from the heat, toss the broccoli, tofu and sesame seeds through the sauce then stir in the spring onions. Divide the chilled dressed noodles between 2 bowls then top with the broccoli and tofu.

NOTES

+ Tofu brings a lovely texture to these noodles, but you can of course use leftover roast chicken, flaked cooked fish or even some edamame beans.
+ Any leftover tofu can be frozen and saved for another meal. The freezing process will change the texture slightly as the tofu loses more water content as it defrosts, but you end up with an even meatier, firmer texture, which is lovely.

Sweet-Soy Omelette, Sushi Rice with quick pickles

Once you get into the swing of making these moreish, slightly sweet Japanese-style omelettes, I reckon they'll soon become part of your weekly cooking routine. It may seem slightly strange asking for broccoli stalk in the pickle, but go with me on it as you get this brilliant crunch that's almost like daikon radish, but easier to source.

Serves 2
Takes 30 minutes

RICE
150g sushi rice
2 tsp rice wine vinegar
½ tsp sea salt flakes
¼ tsp caster sugar
1 tsp sesame oil

QUICK PICKLES
½ garlic clove, finely grated
¼ tsp ginger, finely grated
1½ tsp rice wine vinegar
½ tsp caster sugar
tiny pinch sea salt flakes
¼ tsp Korean red pepper flakes,
    or tiny pinch chilli flakes
1 broccoli stalk, tough end removed
½ carrot

OMELETTES
4 free-range eggs
1 tsp soy sauce, plus extra to serve
1 tsp caster sugar
1 tbsp sesame oil

First, place the rice in a colander then run under the cold water tap for 15-20 seconds until the water from the colander runs clear and no longer milky. Add the drained rice to a small pan with 300ml water then bring it to the boil. Cover with a lid (leave a little bit of space to allow some of the steam to escape) then reduce to a very gentle simmer. Cook for 10 minutes, or until the water has fully absorbed. Remove the pan from the heat.

Meanwhile, in a small bowl, stir together the rice wine vinegar, salt, sugar and sesame oil until mostly dissolved then gently stir this through the cooling rice with a fork and place the lid back on.

Next, make the pickles by stirring the garlic, ginger, rice wine vinegar, sugar, salt and red pepper flakes together in a mixing bowl. Slice up your broccoli stalk and carrot into thin matchsticks then toss in the dressing and set aside to quickly pickle.

To make the omelettes, whisk together the eggs, soy sauce and sugar in a bowl. Drizzle ½ tbsp sesame oil into a frying pan on a high heat. Pour half the whisked egg mixture into the pan then immediately reduce the heat to low. Swirl the pan a few times then, very gently, using a spatula, fold in both sides of the omelette and carefully roll up into a 10cm log (in the same way you would roll a burrito). Once your omelette is golden on the outside, slice it up into 7 or 8 pieces while still in the pan then set aside. Repeat with another ½ tbsp sesame oil and the remaining egg mixture to make a second portion.

Divide up the seasoned rice across 2 bowls, top with the omelette slices and serve up with the pickles. I like to add a tiny splash over my rice at the table to taste, too.

Sweet-Soy Omelette, Sushi Rice and Quick Pickles

NOTES
- If you have some, a sprinkle of togarashi Japanese seasoning is delicious over this dish. You'll find little shakers of it in Asian supermarkets and in most large supermarkets.
- If you need dinner extra fast and have any soba noodles from page 101 left over, make the omelette and pickles and serve with the noodles.
- A tin of good quality tuna dressed in Japanese mayonnaise would be a delicious addition to this meal. You could also add chopped spring onion, pickled sushi ginger, some freshly toasted sesame seeds and a dot of wasabi if you have any.

Soups

Spring Pea and Asparagus Miso Broth
with ricotta dumplings
109

Broken Pasta, Fennel and White Bean Soup
111

Pumpkin and Hazelnut Soup
with Sage-Fried Mushrooms
115

Chickpea and Sun-Dried Tomato Soup
117

Spring Pea and Asparagus Miso Broth with ricotta dumplings

Spring Pea and Asparagus Miso Broth
with ricotta dumplings

I wrote this broth recipe for last year's Spring Series cookery demonstrations to champion the season's asparagus and fresh young alliums. Thanks to the miso and white wine, the broth is bright and uplifting yet still comforting. The ricotta dumplings are dead easy to pull together, but still feel quite fancy and elegant.

Serves 2
Takes 20 minutes, plus 15 minutes for the dumplings

3 radishes
35g butter
1 leek, washed and finely sliced
1 garlic clove, crushed and finely sliced
1 tsp fresh thyme leaves
sea salt flakes
1 tbsp white miso paste
100ml white wine
1 small bunch asparagus
1 handful frozen peas
1 small handful wild garlic, washed
    (use chives if you can't get wild garlic)
good quality extra virgin olive oil to serve

RICOTTA DUMPLINGS
125g ricotta, drained of excess liquid
25g breadcrumbs (shop-bought panko are great)
4 tbsp finely chopped wild garlic (or chives)
zest of ¼ lemon
¼ tsp sea salt flakes

First, slice the radishes as finely as you can then set aside in a bowl of cold water. (You don't need to do this, but it's going to make them curl up beautifully and make you look like a food stylist!).

Heat the butter in a large pan, add the leek, garlic, thyme and a good pinch of salt then gently sauté for 10–12 minutes, ensuring you don't burn the garlic. (You're not looking for colour on the leeks). Add the miso then, using a wooden spoon or spatula, stir it in to help it dissolve. Splash in a little of the wine to further help dissolve the miso, then add the remaining wine and 400ml water. Simmer for 8 minutes or so to cook out the wine.

Meanwhile, make the dumplings by stirring together the ricotta, breadcrumbs, wild garlic, lemon zest and salt. Roll into little dumplings and set aside.

Slice up the asparagus then add to the pan along with the peas and dumplings. Gently cook for 3–4 minutes on a medium heat, then stir in the wild garlic until wilted. Taste for seasoning – you might want to add salt or a squeeze of lemon. Serve up between 2 bowls, topped with the radish and a drizzle of your best olive oil.

NOTES

+ If making this for a crowd, pre-cook the dumplings by simmering them in a pan of stock or water for a few minutes then remove with a slotted spoon a few hours before eating. When ready to serve, simply divide between bowls and pour over the hot broth.

Broken Pasta, Fennel and White Bean Soup

Not many weeks go by when I don't make a variation on this minestrone-type soup as it's ideal for using up anything that has been left to wilt at the bottom of the fridge. So feel free to throw in any extra veg that I haven't listed below.

If we don't have any odds and ends of pasta to use up, often I'll make sourdough croutons to soak up the soup instead – just delicious.

Serves 4
Takes 1 hour

1 large carrot
1 stick celery
1 onion or bunch of spring onions
1 fennel
4 tbsp olive oil
    (or oil from a jar of sun-dried tomatoes)
3 bay leaves
½ tsp fennel seeds
tiny pinch chilli flakes (or more to taste)
2 tsp sea salt, plus extra to taste
(1 Parmesan rind, optional)
1 tbsp tomato purée
1 × 400g tin plum tomatoes
¼ tsp caster sugar
200ml white wine
140g pasta (any shape will do, or it can be an
    assortment of odds and ends)
1 × 400g tin cannellini beans
1 large handful cabbage, cavolo nero or kale
    (approx 100g)
1 large handful flat-leaf parsley (approx 20g)

First, finely slice the carrot, celery, onion and fennel; setting aside the fennel fronds for garnishing later. Heat the oil on high in a large, deep pan then throw in the veg along with the bay, fennel seeds, chilli flakes, salt (and Parmesan rind, if using). Fry on a high heat for 10 minutes, stirring occasionally so that it all gains some beautiful colour. Meanwhile, boil a full kettle.

Stir the tomato purée into the vegetables then fry for 2 minutes before adding the tomatoes and sugar, crushing the tomatoes with your hands as you pour them in. Pour in the wine (I half fill the tin of tomatoes to roughly measure out the wine and slosh out any last tomato juices) and 750ml boiling water. Break any large pasta into bite-sized pieces then throw into the pot (or leave the pasta whole if using smaller shapes). Drain the beans (I use the tin lid as a colander), then pour them into the pan, using your hands to crush the last handful of beans as the bean starches will encourage the soup to thicken. Boil for 15 minutes, stirring occasionally to ensure no pasta gets stuck to the bottom of the pan.

Shred up your cabbage then add to the soup and boil for a further 10 minutes. Remove from the heat then allow the soup to sit and relax for 5 minutes. Roughly chop the parsley, stir it into the soup then taste for seasoning. Serve up with the reserved fennel fronds or with the breadcrumbs (page 84), aioli (page 19) or salsa verde on page 21.

NOTES

+ We always work through lots of Parmesan in our house, so I often keep hold of the rind in a little tub in the fridge and drop them into recipes like this, or into chicken soups, ragu or noodle broths for added seasoning and umami flavour.
+ You can of course substitute red wine for white here, but I prefer the lightness of white. Cider makes an excellent swap, too.
+ I've listed flat-leaf parsley, but throw in any soft herbs that need using up: dill, tarragon, basil etc.

Broken Pasta, Fennel and White Bean Soup

Pumpkin and Hazelnut Soup with sage-fried mushrooms

Pumpkin and Hazelnut Soup
with sage-fried mushrooms

It feels incredibly clichéd to say this is autumn in a bowl... but that's exactly what this is! The better your pumpkin and mushrooms here, the better your soup, so try and hunt down a kabocha squash (sometimes called Japanese pumpkin) or delica pumpkin and some wild mushrooms if you can. Failing that, a supermarket butternut squash and some button mushrooms will still give you a delicious supper. The magic comes from the sage that becomes all crispy when fried in butter. Hello, autumn.

Serves 6
Takes 1 hour 15 minutes, but most of that is hands-off oven time

SOUP
3 white onions
1 medium pumpkin or butternut squash
    (approx 1.1kg)
4 baby potatoes (approx 215g)
5 tbsp olive oil or cold-pressed rapeseed oil
2 tsp sea salt flakes, plus extra to taste
100g blanched hazelnuts
100ml white wine
1 garlic clove

MUSHROOMS
90g salted butter
12 shitake, wild or chestnut mushrooms
    (approx 180g), roughly torn
20 sage leaves, roughly torn
black pepper

First, preheat the oven to 200°C (400°F/gas 6) and line a really large baking tray with baking paper. (I use the tray that comes included with the oven.) Peel the onions and cut them into chunky wedges. Halve and remove the seeds from the pumpkin (I don't bother peeling the pumpkin skin as life is too short), then cut into small dice. Quarter the potatoes (again, I don't bother peeling them); then place them along with the onions and pumpkin onto the lined baking tray, toss in 4 tbsp oil and 2 tsp salt, and bake for 40 minutes, tossing half-way through.

Remove the tray from the oven, give the vegetables another toss as they should have caramelised at some of the edges by now, then free up a corner of the tray and add in the hazelnuts. Roast for another 7–8 minutes, or until the hazelnuts are a deep golden brown colour.

Meanwhile, boil a full kettle.

Transfer the roasted vegetables and hazelnuts to a large soup pan then cover with 1.2 litres of boiling water and the wine. Bring to the boil then simmer on high with a lid on for 5 minutes. Remove from the heat.

Using a hand blender, blitz until completely smooth. (The next step may sound slighlty weird, but just trust me!) Throw the peeled raw garlic clove and 1 tbsp oil into the soup then blend once again until completely emulsified and extra velvety. Taste for seasoning then prepare the mushrooms.

Heat the butter on a high heat in a frying pan. Throw in the torn mushrooms, sage, and a very generous amount of freshly cracked black pepper. Fry for 3–4 minutes until caramelised at the edges and really fragrant, stirring regularly.

To serve, spoon a few ladlefuls of soup into a bowl, then top with the fried mushrooms and every last drop of that sage-infused butter.

NOTES
+ A few chilli flakes and some lemon zest on top of the mushrooms and soup is also nice – but that's a move that applies to pretty much all of my cooking!

Chickpea and Sun-Dried Tomato Soup

A jar of sun-dried tomatoes is an incredibly handy thing to keep in your fridge. I often use the infused jar oil for frying vegetables, and here they add punch to a comforting chickpea soup, without the acidity that a tin of chopped tomatoes brings. There's a comforting familiarity about this soup, it reminds me of the lentil soup my mum would pack me off to school with, but with added layers of flavour.

Serves 2, plus a toddler, and a portion for the freezer or lunch the next day
Takes 45 minutes

3 tbsp olive oil or cold-pressed rapeseed oil
1 white onion, peeled and finely sliced
2 sticks celery, finely sliced
1 large carrot, peeled and finely sliced
¼ tsp sea salt flakes, plus extra to taste
1 chicken or vegetable stock cube (I like Kallo)
1 × 400g tin chickpeas
1 garlic clove (peeled)
5 sun-dried tomatoes, plus 1 for garnish
1 small handful flat-leaf parsley (approx 10g)
pinch chilli flakes
½ tsp lemon juice

Heat the oil in a large soup pot over a high heat then add the onion, celery, carrot and salt. Fry for 12–15 minutes until turning golden and really fragrant, stirring occasionally to stop the vegetables catching. Meanwhile, boil the kettle then dissolve the stock cube in 500ml boiling water.

Add the stock to the pan along with the tin of chickpeas, including the tin juices, then boil for 3–4 minutes. Remove from the heat then, using a hand blender, blitz with the garlic (don't worry that it's raw, it will mellow and be delicious, I promise!) and sun-dried tomatoes until smooth.

To make the topping, finely chop the extra sun-dried tomato with the parsley and a pinch of chilli flakes on your chopping board. Transfer to a small bowl then stir in the lemon juice. Taste for seasoning, then taste the soup for seasoning, ensuring you have a lovely balance between both.

Ladle the soup into bowls then spoon over the herby sun-dried tomato topping.

NOTES
+ You can definitely swap the chickpeas for any tinned or jarred beans or pulses.
+ Likewise, substitute the flat-leaf parsley for any soft herbs you have in your fridge that need using up. Olives and capers are a delicious addition to the herby topping too.
+ Once blended, this soup is great for freezing for up to a month. So a great one for scaling up then storing in smaller portions.

Chickpea and Sun-Dried Tomato Soup

Meat and Fish

Tuna, Egg and Baby Potato Salad
with green beans, shallots and capers
123

Wild Garlic and Sausage Meatballs
Cooked in Milk and Lemon
with chickpea and olive oil mash
125

Tarragon and Garlic Roast Chicken,
Potatoes and Cavolo Nero
129

Chicken Schnitzel with Crispy Capers,
Rosemary and Lemon
133

Fish Baps with herby peas and tartare sauce
135

Tuna, Egg and Baby Potato Salad with green beans, shallots and capers

Tuna, Egg and Baby Potato Salad
with green beans, shallots and capers

This *sort-of* Niçoise salad is exactly what I want to eat out in the garden in the warmer months. Ideally with a cold glass of wine and plenty of fresh baguette to hand. You can leave the tuna out altogether if you like: the egg alone is satisfying enough, or if you have a bit more time on a weekend, serve this salad with a garlicky roast chicken.

Serves 2
Takes 20 minutes

350g baby potatoes
1 tsp sea salt flakes, plus ¼ tsp
2 free-range eggs
85g green beans, trimmed
1 shallot or ½ onion (45g)
1 tbsp cider vinegar
1 tbsp capers
¼ tsp caster sugar
2 tsp Dijon mustard
1 tbsp cold-pressed rapeseed oil
1 × 112g tin great quality white tuna in oil
    (I like Ortiz)
black pepper

First, boil a half-full kettle. Halve and/or quarter the potatoes then place them in a medium pan with 1 tsp salt. Cover with boiling water then simmer on high for 9 minutes, add the eggs, then cook for a further 7 minutes. Fish out the eggs, then add the green beans to the pan and simmer for 2 minutes. Peel the eggs as the beans are cooking (I have asbestos fingers, but run the eggs under cold water for a few seconds to make them easier to handle if you like.) Drain the potatoes and eggs in a colander and allow to steam dry.

Meanwhile, peel and slice the shallot into rounds as finely as you can. Add them to a large mixing bowl, toss in ¼ tsp salt, the vinegar, capers and sugar, then scrunch the shallots with your fingers to help them lightly pickle.

Once the potatoes and green beans are draining in the colander, stir the mustard and oil into the shallots, toss in the potatoes and green beans to nicely dress them, then divide between 2 plates.

Halve the tuna and eggs over each plate then grind over lots of black pepper. Enjoy whilst still slightly warm.

NOTES

+ Any soft herbs like parsley, dill and tarragon are a great finisher for the salad, a bit of lemon zest to finish is always a good idea too.
+ If you can, try to get your hands on a really good crusty baguette to eat with this so that you can mop up the shallot and caper dressing.
+ Tuna is quite a treat in our house as I'm very conscious that it's not the most sustainable option. I try to opt for a higher-quality line and pole-caught brand and would rather have good-quality, juicy tuna occasionally as a treat than cheaper, watery tuna more often.

Wild Garlic and Sausage Meatballs Cooked in Milk and Lemon
with chickpea and olive oil mash

Back when I had Elliott's Cafe, these meatballs would go onto the menu blackboard as soon as the wild garlic arrived – they were always a hit. The lemon and milk are going to combine and curdle slightly to give you the most deliciously creamy, herb-infused sauce to spoon over the chickpea mash. So don't worry if they feel like slightly unusual ingredients to cook your meatballs in compared to, say, a tomato sauce. This dish is all about celebrating just how delicious beige food can be.

I suggest making plenty of these meatballs as they're very crowd-pleasing and I find they always disappear quickly! Just swap the wild garlic for some other greenery once the season is over. If it's not in season or you can't get wild garlic, just substitute it for 15g flat-leaf parsley and 1 finely grated garlic clove.

Serves 2
Takes 30 minutes

MEATBALLS
1 handful wild garlic (15g), washed and patted dry, plus 15g for the sauce
10g Parmesan cheese
1 lemon
4 pork sausages (250g meat once skins removed)
1 tbsp vegetable, rapeseed or olive oil
8 sage leaves
200ml milk (ideally whole)

CHICKPEA MASH
1 × 400g tin chickpeas
3 tbsp good extra virgin olive oil, plus extra for drizzling
¼ tsp sea salt flakes

Wild Garlic and Sausage Meatballs Cooked in Milk and Lemon with chickpea and olive oil mash

First, make the meatballs. Finely chop the wild garlic, then add it to a mixing bowl (or parsley and garlic, if substituting with those). Use a microplane to finely grate all of the Parmesan and half of the lemon's peel (save the rest of the lemon peel for frying), then add both to the bowl. Remove the sausages from their skins (discard the skins), then add the meat to the bowl. Wet your hands then squeeze the mixture together until well combined. Roll out 14 small meatballs, between 15-20g each in weight.

Heat the oil in a large frying pan on a medium-high heat, then use a speed peeler to peel off small strips of the remaining lemon skin. Throw this into the pan along with the sage leaves and meatballs, then fry on a medium heat for 5 minutes. You're looking to build a golden brown colour on all sides of the meatballs, and as the pork fat renders the sage and lemon peel should crisp up and become really aromatic. Pour in the milk, 2 tsp lemon juice and the extra handful of wild garlic (if you've got it). Simmer for 5 minutes, stirring occasionally. The sauce will curdle but please don't worry: it will be really delicious and it's texture you're aiming for here. Check the meatballs are cooked through in the middle, then taste the sauce for seasoning.

Meanwhile, to make the chickpea mash, drain the liquid from the tin (I just use the tin lid for this rather than having to wash a colander), then add to a medium pan with the extra virgin olive oil and salt. Warm gently on a medium heat for 2 minutes then, using a hand blender, blitz until you have a thick hummus consistency. Return to a very low heat for a further minute. Taste both the chickpea mash and the meatball sauce for seasoning, then divide up between 2 bowls with any remaining lemons you have cut into wedges.

NOTES

+ As the meatballs and mash are such a beautifully beige combination, I like to serve a bitter radicchio or green salad and punchy wild garlic aioli dressing alongside.

+ If you can't get your hands on wild garlic, you could throw a handful of spinach leaves into the meatball sauce for a few minutes until wilted before serving.
+ If you like, you can test the seasoning of your meatball mix by frying off a tiny little bit and having a taste before rolling them all out. I find the Parmesan alone seasons the meatballs enough, plus the sauce becomes quite salty and concentrated as it cooks, so I don't add extra salt myself.
+ If you're using a pack of 6 sausages and want to use them all up, just make extra meatballs and have them in a sandwich the next day – delicious!

Tarragon and Garlic Roast Chicken, Potatoes and Cavolo Nero

This is my sped-up version of Julius Roberts' magnificent tarragon roast chicken (his book *The Farm Table* is a joy and I'd highly recommend getting a copy). Julius uses a whole bird, but I like to use chicken thighs rather than roasting a bird midweek. The mustard, capers and shallot cut through the tarragon cream and make the most sensational sauce.

I've specifically written this up with leftovers sandwiches the next day in mind, as it really does make for the best sarnies. White bloomer bread, please!

Serves 2, with leftovers for chicken sandwiches the next day
Takes 1 hour, but very little hands-on time

350g baby potatoes
6 boneless chicken thighs (700g)
    skin on or off, depending on your preference
½ tsp sea salt
1 tbsp good olive oil
4 garlic cloves
1 large handful tarragon (15g)
100ml double cream
75ml white wine
2½ tsp Dijon mustard
1 tbsp capers
½ lemon
1 tsp lemon juice, plus 1 tsp for the cavolo nero
black pepper
1 shallot
100g cavolo nero

First, preheat the oven to 200°C (400°F/gas 6). Cut the potatoes into quarters (don't bother peeling them),

Tarragon and Garlic Roast Chicken, Potatoes and Cavolo Nero

place on a medium baking tray, then put the chicken on top, (skin-side up.) Coat the potatoes and chicken in the salt and olive oil, then place the garlic cloves under the chicken. You don't need to peel or crush the garlic as they'll steam in their own skins. Roast for 30 minutes.

Meanwhile, strip the tarragon leaves off the stalks then stir in a small bowl with the cream, wine, mustard and capers. Use a microplane to finely zest in the lemon, then squeeze in 1 tsp lemon juice. Crack in loads of black pepper then stir to combine. Pour this over the chicken and potatoes then bake for a further 10 minutes. Peel and finely dice the shallot, stir this into the cream and tray juices, then bake for a final 5 minutes.

Meanwhile, chop the cavolo nero, including the stems, into 1½ cm slices, then simmer in a small pan of boiling water for 2 minutes. Drain well in a colander.

Divide up most of the chicken, the potatoes and cavolo nero between 2 plates, ensuring you spoon over loads of those incredible tray juices, not forgetting the roasted garlic. I like to squeeze a bit of fresh lemon juice over the cavolo nero too to cut through the cream. Any leftover chicken and sauce will make the most incredible leftovers sandwiches – see notes below.

>SANDWICHES THE NEXT DAY FOR 2 PEOPLE
>4 slices white bloomer or sourdough bread
>leftover chicken, sliced
>2 cornichons or jalapeños, finely sliced
>a few baby gem leaves
>1 ripe tomato, sliced
>Worcestershire sauce

Rather than buttering your bread, spread over any leftover creamy pan juices, then layer up with chicken, cornichons/jalapeños, lettuce, tomato and a few splashes of Worcestershire sauce. Delicious!

Chicken Schnitzel with Crispy Capers, Rosemary and Lemon

Chicken Schnitzel with Crispy Capers, Rosemary and Lemon

My family always gets so excited when I say it's chicken schnitzel for dinner. I think it's a nostalgic, comforting dish for many of us, isn't it?

I make a plain version for Nora (she's only 2!), but then add crispy capers, rosemary and lemon to mine and Philip's to elevate the flavours and textures. If I was making this for a Studio event I would probably marinade the chicken in buttermilk for a few hours to make it extra special, but I'm never organised enough to do that at home. The option is there, though!

Serves 2
Takes 30 minutes

40g plain flour
1 free-range egg
1 tsp Dijon mustard
½ tsp paprika
½ tsp sea salt flakes
50g panko breadcrumbs
15g Parmesan cheese, finely grated
zest of ½ lemon
2 chicken breasts
5 tbsp cold-pressed rapeseed or vegetable oil
1 tbsp capers
2 rosemary stalks, leaves stripped,
    stalks discarded
pinch chilli flakes

First, set up 3 separate deep plates for breading your chicken. Measure out your flour on the first plate. Whisk the egg and mustard together in the second. Stir the paprika, salt, breadcrumbs, Parmesan and lemon zest together on the third plate.

Next, butterfly each chicken breast by cutting an incision down the middle and opening it out like a book. Place a breast between two sheets of baking paper then bash with a rolling pin on a board until 1cm thick. Repeat with the second chicken breast then pass each through the flour, egg and breadcrumbs; then set aside to get ready for frying.

Heat the oil in a frying pan on a high heat then, taking care, gently lay the chicken in the pan (lay it away from you, so there's less chance of splashing yourself in hot oil!). Fry for 3–4 minutes until dark golden, then carefully using a fish slice or tongs, flip the chicken and repeat for the other side. Flip again and cook for further 30 seconds on each side, by which point it should be a deep golden brown.

Test that one of the schnitzels is fully cooked in the middle, then transfer to a plate lined with kitchen paper.

Reduce the pan heat to low, then throw in the capers, rosemary and chilli flakes, fry for a minute until crispy and aromatic, then spoon over the schnitzels. Cut the lemon into wedges for squeezing over, too.

Fish Baps
with herby peas and tartare sauce

If you've mastered the breadcrumbing process for the chicken schnitzels, then you'll find making these fish baps an absolute doddle. You could add some homemade chips if you wanted to, but I find these pretty filling as they are. Try and chat to your fishmonger about what's the most sustainable fish option if you can, pollock is my favourite choice if they have it.

Takes 25 minutes
Serves 2 very generously (we like to eat 'samples'
of the fish as we're cooking!)

2 × cod/pollock/coley loin fillets, skin and boneless
40g plain flour
1 free-range egg
1 lemon
10g Parmesan cheese
45g panko breadcrumbs
5 tbsp cold-pressed rapeseed oil or vegetable oil
sea salt flakes
2 white bread rolls

HERBY PEAS
150g frozen peas
½ tsp lemon juice
1 small handful of dill/parsley or both (10g)

TARTARE SAUCE
1 tbsp capers
½ shallot or ¼ onion
2 tbsp mayonnaise
1 tbsp natural yoghurt
½ tsp Dijon mustard
½ tsp lemon juice
(a few splashes of Worcestershire sauce, optional)

First, half fill and boil a kettle. Pat the fish dry with plenty of kitchen paper, then slice into 5cm-ish chunks. Allow any excess moisture to continue soaking into a few more top sheets of kitchen paper whilst you prep the peas and the tartare sauce.

Cover the peas in a small pan of boiling water then allow to sit for 2 minutes. I don't bother cooking them as such, as they stay nice and fresh this way. Drain in a colander, then return the peas back to the pan. Squeeze in the lemon juice, tear in the herbs, then using a hand blender, pulse until you have a chunky pea purée.

Finely chop the capers and shallot or onion, then add to a small bowl and stir in the mayo, yoghurt, Dijon and lemon juice. Taste for seasoning. If you want more of a 'burger sauce' flavour, then splash in some Worcestershire sauce.

Set up 3 separate deep plates for your fish. Measure out your flour on the first plate. Whisk the egg in the second. Zest the lemon, finely grate the Parmesan then stir into the breadcrumbs on the third plate. Pass each piece of fish through the flour, egg and breadcrumbs then set aside to get ready for frying.

Heat the oil in a frying pan on a high heat then, taking care, gently lay in each piece of fish (lay the fish away from you, so there's less chance of splashing yourself in hot oil!). Fry for 3-4 minutes until dark golden, then carefully using a fish slice, flip the pieces of fish and repeat for the other side. Test that one of the pieces is fully cooked in the middle, then transfer to a plate lined with kitchen paper and sprinkle with sea salt.

Layer up the rolls with tartare, peas and your beautifully cooked fish, then tuck in. We tend to get the bottle of tomato ketchup out at this point, too!

Fish Baps with herby peas and tartare sauce

Puddings

School Dinner Chocolate Pudding
141

Marmalade Toast Sponge Pudding
143

Lemon Madeleines
146

Treacle Fig Tea Loaf
151

Earl Grey Prune Clafoutis
153

Brown-Butter and Rosemary Apple Cake
157

Morning Cake for Coffee
161

Blackcurrant Fool
163

School Dinner Chocolate Pudding

School Dinner Chocolate Pudding

This is not the fanciest dessert in my repertoire, but oh, how it hits the spot when you need a bit of nostalgic comfort! Similar to what we had at school (but without the lumpy custard), this sponge pudding only uses cocoa powder and a few store-cupboard basics. We never have chocolate as an ingredient in our house as it just gets eaten!

Go with me when it comes to pouring the boiling water mixture over the sponge – it feels like a slightly strange thing to do, but you end up with a self-saucing pudding. Also, every oven is different so use the baking times below as a guideline only: you're looking for the sponge to be cooked in the middle with a large pool of chocolate sauce. Take a peek after 12 minutes in case your oven runs extra hot. Under-baked is better than over-baked here.

Serves 2 very generously, or you could serve 4 people in small bowls if adding cream or ice-cream as it's very rich
Takes 5 minutes, plus 15 minutes baking time

SPONGE PUDDING
30g butter
75g self-raising flour
½ tsp baking powder
tiny pinch sea salt flakes
35g dark brown sugar
20g cocoa powder
1 free-range egg
45ml milk (ideally whole)
(double cream or ice cream to serve, optional)

CHOCOLATE SAUCE
35g dark brown sugar
10g cocoa powder

First, preheat the oven to 160°C (320°F/gas 3) then pop the kettle on (you'll only need 65ml boiling water for the chocolate sauce, so it doesn't need to be a full kettle).

Cut the butter into small cubes then place in a small dish – the one I use is a small traditional pie dish that we sell at Elliott's. Place the dish in the oven for a minute or two as the oven warms up to gently melt the butter. Use a pastry brush to grease the sides of the dish, then set aside. (If your butter seems crazy hot, then allow it to cool for a few minutes by transferring it to another bowl. This is to prevent the butter from scrambling the egg that you'll be adding shortly, but I don't usually need to do this).

Whisk together the self-raising flour, baking powder, salt, brown sugar and cocoa powder in a large bowl, then stir in the melted butter. Crack in the egg, pour in the milk, then stir until you have a smooth batter. Scrape the batter into the buttered baking dish.

In the same bowl you used to mix the batter (to save on washing up!), make the sauce by stirring together the dark brown sugar, cocoa powder and 65ml boiling water until smooth. Pour it over the batter (this sounds a bit strange, but just go with me!) then bake for 16 minutes.

Remove the pudding from the oven, allow it to sit for 1 minute, where it will continue to firm up, then serve up and tuck in, ideally with plenty of cold cream!

NOTES
+ When making the sauce, feel free to add ½ tsp instant espresso powder if mocha flavour is your kind of thing.
+ Don't worry if you only have plain flour and not self-raising, just up the baking powder to 1 tsp.

Marmalade Toast Sponge Pudding

You might have seen me making this marmalade pudding before as it's one of my absolute favourites, and there's no way it wasn't getting a spot in this book as it's so quick and easy to bake midweek.

Lazy mornings in PJs with the radio on, a pot of coffee to share with my husband and several rounds of marmalade on toast is the inspiration for this ridiculously good pudding. For me, pumpernickel rye bread makes the tastiest sponge, but use any bread you've got that needs eating. Just be sure to add plenty of double cream!

Serves 2
Takes 15 minutes,
plus 30–35 minutes baking time

65g salted butter,
    plus a tiny knob for greasing the dish
25g sourdough or pumpernickel rye bread
40g soft brown sugar
70g marmalade, plus 2 tablespoons for the glaze
40g plain flour
¼ tsp baking powder
1 free-range egg
small pinch sea salt flakes
zest of 1 orange
double cream to serve

Preheat the oven to 180°C (350°F/gas 4) and, using your fingers, grease the base and sides of your dish with butter. (I use the same dish that I use for the chocolate pudding and it measures 18cm × 12.5cm × 6cm).

Cut the bread into rough chunks, place in a food processor and blitz to fine breadcrumbs. Add the remaining butter, sugar, marmalade, flour, baking powder, egg, salt and orange zest, then pulse until combined. (You can carefully use a box grater to crush the bread into crumbs and then beat everything with a wooden spoon in a large bowl until smooth too, if you prefer).

Scrape the batter into the buttered dish and bake in the preheated oven for 30–35 minutes, or until deep golden. Remove from the oven and leave to cool slightly in the dish.

Meanwhile, place 2 tbsp marmalade in a small saucepan with 2 tablespoons of water. Warm over a high heat for 2–3 minutes, stirring regularly with a wooden spoon, until you have a syrupy glaze full of orange shreds.

Pour the marmalade glaze over the top of the sponge, allow it to sink in for a minute or two, then serve up with plenty of cold double cream.

Marmalade Toast Sponge Pudding

Lemon Madeleines

I know not every kitchen includes a madeleine tin as standard, but I recommend you buy one for making these alone as they're ridiculously easy and feel so chic. I reckon you'll be amazed by how quickly a batch of these comes together. No longer just the preserve of fancy restaurants!

Makes 12 madeleines
Takes 10 minutes, plus 12 minutes baking time

100g unsalted butter,
    plus 1 tbsp for buttering the tin
100g plain flour, plus more for dusting the tins
1 tbsp honey
1 lemon, zested, plus another lemon for garnish
100g caster sugar
2 free-range eggs
¾ tsp baking powder

Preheat the oven to 180°C (350°F/gas 4). Gently melt the butter in a small pan, remove from the heat then liberally brush the tin with the melted butter. Dust the greased tin with flour, tap out any excess, then place in the freezer. This is going to ensure your madeleines don't stick to the tin.

Stir the honey and lemon zest into the melted butter. In a bowl, stir together the caster sugar and eggs until smooth, then stir in the melted butter mixture.

In another bowl, whisk together the flour and baking powder. Stir this mixture into the egg and butter mixture until smooth. Spoon the batter into the madeleine tin.

Bake for 10–12 minutes, or until they have formed a peak in the middle, and are lightly golden.

Remove from the oven, then use a teaspoon or small knife to remove them from the tin. Zest over the lemon.

Lemon Madeleines

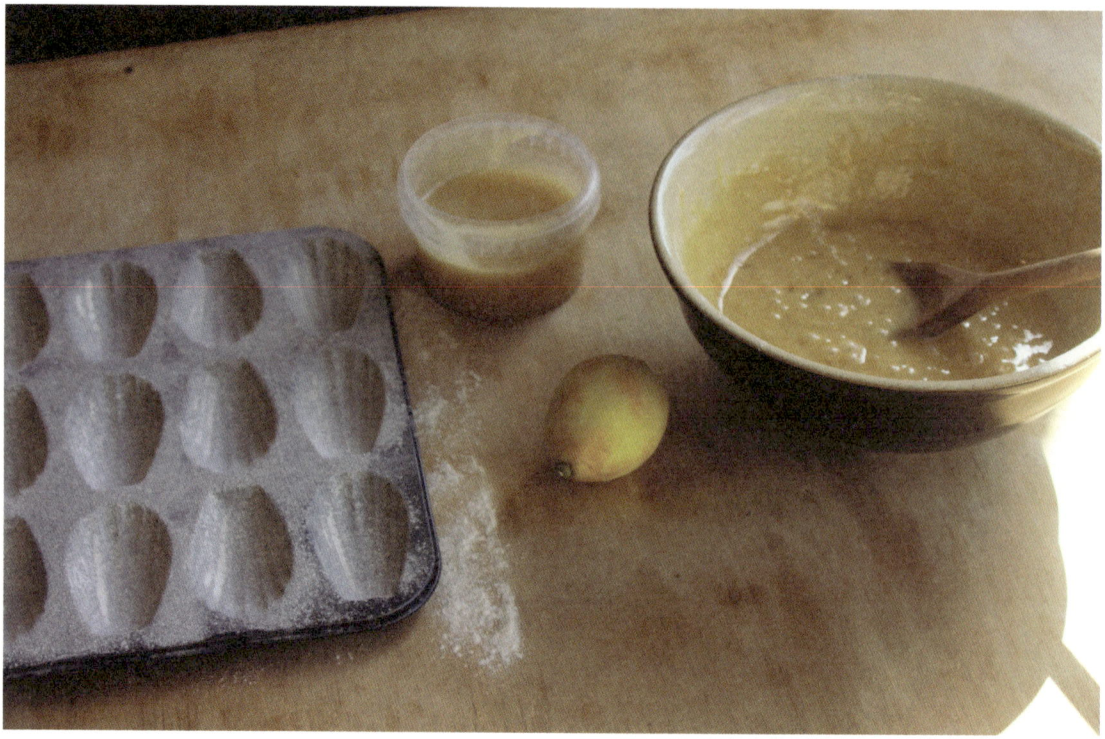

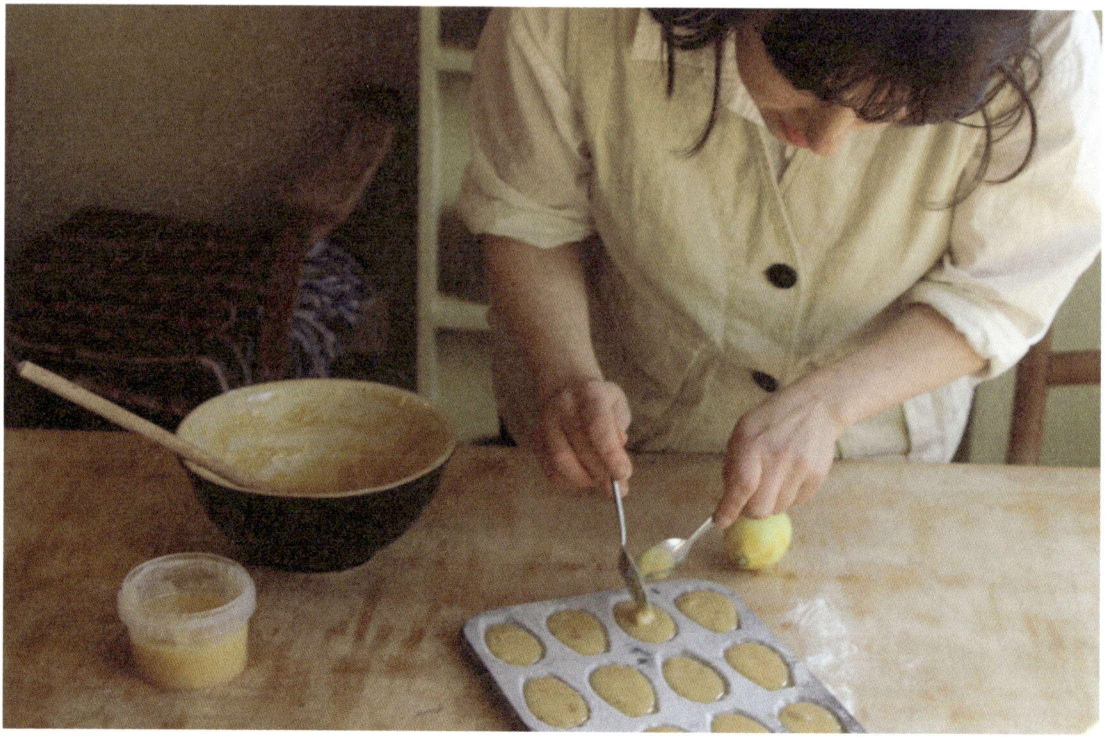

Lemon Madeleines

NOTES

+ These are best when eaten fresh and warm, which is why restaurants ask you to order them at the start of your meal. You can keep the batter in the fridge for up to 2 days then bake off a few madeleines at a time if you like. Just keep it in a well-sealed container.

Treacle Fig Tea Loaf

Treacle Fig Tea Loaf

This squidgy loaf was such a hit when I sent it out for blind recipe testing. Somewhere between a bread and a cake and packed with tea-soaked figs, seeds and oats; it feels very British in a really good way. The kind of thing to keep in a tin and pull out at elevenses to have with a pot of tea or coffee. (Oh, how I love the concept of elevenses!)

You'll see in the notes that I suggest trying a slice of this loaf with cheese, trust me on this one, it's such a great combination.

Makes 1 loaf
Takes 15 minutes, plus 1 hour baking time

2 × English breakfast tea bags
160g dried figs
50g runny honey
100g treacle
125g dark brown sugar
200g plain flour
1 tsp baking powder
80g rolled oats
75g mixed seeds,
    plus extra for sprinkling on top
pinch sea salt flakes
2 free-range eggs

Preheat the oven to 160°C (320°F/gas 3).

Boil the kettle – it doesn't need to be full, just enough to make a really strong bowl of tea with the tea bags and 125ml boiling water. Remove the stems from the figs, finely slice, then place them in the bowl of tea. Allow to soak while you line a loaf tin with baking paper. My loaf tin measures 20cm × 13cm × 9cm.

Gently warm the honey, treacle and dark brown sugar in a small pan until melted and combined. Remove from the heat and allow to cool slightly.

Treacle Fig Tea Loaf

Whisk together the flour, baking powder, oats, seeds and salt in a mixing bowl to ensure the baking powder is well distributed. Stir in the figs and their liquid (discarding the teabags). Make a little well, crack in the eggs, then lightly whisk to break them. Pour in the slightly cooled treacle mixture then stir until everything is well combined.

Pour the batter into the lined loaf tin, top with more seeds, then bake for 55–60 minutes or until springy. A skewer inserted into the middle of the loaf should come out clean when it's done. Allow to cool in the tin before slicing up and serving.

NOTES
+ As it's so sticky, this loaf keeps well in a tin for up to 4 days.
+ We love eating it with Parmesan, mature Cheddar or a mountain-style cheese.
+ I freeze chunks of the loaf for a month or so.

Earl Grey Prune Clafoutis

Have you ever tried a canelé (the little fluted custardy French pastries) before? They are my all-time favourite treat, but quite a technical faff to make as you need copper moulds lined with beeswax and a fussy batter that rests overnight. Well, this clafoutis is my dead-easy version for getting those divine canelé flavours in a family friendly, just-mix-then-throw-it-in-the-oven-type pudding.

I featured this recipe at my Winter Series of cookery demonstrations last year and managed to convert all of the prune haters in the room! With minimal effort, you get such a great pudding here that can be adapted throughout the seasons: just swap the prunes for whichever fruit is best. Cherries, peaches and rhubarb all work brilliantly.

Serves 4
Takes 15 minutes, plus 30 minutes baking time

3 tbsp loose leaf Earl Grey tea
250g pitted prunes
35g salted butter
tiny pinch sea salt flakes
70g dark brown sugar
100g plain flour
4 free-range eggs
½ tsp baking powder
½ tsp vanilla bean paste
a few grindings of black pepper
(splash of rum, optional)
200ml whole milk
2 tbsp Demerara sugar
1 tbsp icing sugar, for dusting
(double cream and candied orange peel to serve, optional)

Earl Grey Prune Clafoutis

Preheat the oven to 200°C/400°F/gas 6. Brew the Earl Grey with 160ml boiling water in a jug or teapot for 5 minutes. Then, using a small strainer, pour 50ml tea over the prunes in a bowl and set aside.

Place the butter in a 23cm round cake tin or baking dish, bake for 3–4 minutes to turn golden, then spread over the base and sides using a pastry brush or spatula.

Tip the soaked prunes (and Earl Grey juices) into the tin or dish, placing on a baking tray to catch any potential drips.

In a large bowl, whisk together the salt, dark brown sugar, flour, eggs, baking powder, vanilla bean paste, pepper (and rum, if using) until smooth. Gradually stir in the milk until combined, then pour the batter over the prunes. Sprinkle over the Demerara sugar, then bake for 30 minutes, until golden.

Dust with icing sugar and serve warm with plenty of cold double cream and candied peel, if you like.

NOTES
+ You can make this clafoutis with any berries, cherries or stone fruit, depending on what's in season. If using frozen berries, just bake for 10 minutes before pouring over the batter.

Brown-Butter and Rosemary Apple Cake

Brown-Butter and Rosemary Apple Cake

I shared this recipe on Instagram last autumn, and it's been the most recreated recipe that I've ever written, so I thought it would be lovely to include in print here as it's so simple to bake, even midweek.

Browning the butter with rosemary doesn't make the cake 'soapy' at all, so please don't be scared, you just get this incredibly fragrant sponge that complements the apples and almonds beautifully. Tag me if you make this one and I'll add you to the saved album...

Serves 8
Takes 20 minutes, plus 45 minutes baking time

6 sprigs rosemary
200g salted butter
225g self-raising flour
1 tsp baking powder
225g soft brown sugar
2 free-range eggs
(3 tbsp rum, optional)
300g cooking apples, peeled and cored
50g flaked almonds

Place the rosemary and butter in a pan, then heat on medium for 4–5 minutes, stirring regularly. You're looking for the butter to foam up and turn golden before turning dark brown. A few dark specks will appear and sit on the base of the pan and it'll smell really nutty. Drain through a fine sieve, discarding the rosemary, then allow to cool gently. It doesn't matter if the odd bit of rosemary is still in the butter.

Preheat the oven to 160°C (320°F/gas 3). Lightly grease a deep 23cm loose-bottomed cake tin and line with greaseproof paper.

Measure the flour, baking powder, sugar, eggs, rum (if using) into a bowl and add the melted-but-slightly-cooled butter. Mix well with a wooden spoon until completely combined. It'll feel very thick for a cake batter, but this is correct – don't worry.

Spread half of this mixture in the prepared tin. Thickly slice the apples and lay on top of the mixture in the tin, piling mostly towards the centre. Spoon the remaining mixture over the apples. This is an awkward thing to do, but just make sure that the mixture covers the centre well as it will spread out in the oven.

Sprinkle with the almonds and bake in the preheated oven for 45 minutes to 1 hour until golden and coming away from the sides of the tin.

NOTES
+ You can make this cake the day ahead, just keep it well-covered.
+ I love serving this with crème fraîche to cut through the richness of the butter.
+ Feel free to play with substituting the rosemary for other woody herbs like sage and thyme.

Brown-Butter and Rosemary Apple Cake

Morning Cake for Coffee

Morning Cake for Coffee

Inspired by the beautifully simple breakfast cakes you find across Italy, for me, this is the perfect bake to enjoy with a strong espresso. The secret to the golden crumb is cold-pressed rapeseed oil or vibrant green light olive oil, but regular sunflower or vegetable oil works too.

>150ml cold-pressed rapeseed oil,
>   plus 1 tsp for greasing
>250g plain flour
>250g caster sugar
>3 tsp baking powder
>150g natural yoghurt
>grated zest of 1 lemon
>grated zest of ½ grapefruit or ½ orange
>1 tsp vanilla paste
>3 free-range eggs
>2 tbsp icing sugar, for dusting

Preheat the oven to 180°C (350°F/gas 4). Using a pastry brush, grease a 23cm springform cake tin with oil.

Next, place the flour, sugar and baking powder in a large mixing bowl. Using a fork or balloon whisk, thoroughly mix together to ensure the baking powder is evenly distributed.

Throw in the yoghurt, oil, citrus zests and vanilla. Crack in the eggs and then stir until just combined. Pour the batter into the greased tin and bake for 35 minutes, or until springy to the touch.

While still warm, turn out the cake onto a large plate and, using a small sieve, dust with the icing sugar. Allow to cool for 10 minutes.

>NOTES
> + This cake keeps well for a couple of days when stored in an airtight container.

Blackcurrant Fool

Blackcurrant Fool

We're spoilt for blackcurrants in our garden, and aside from my blackcurrant-leaf custard pavlova (which I'll write up in a book of weekend recipes for when you've got more time in the kitchen), this fool is my favourite way to celebrate them.

This cream fool is tart, light and elegant enough to be on the pudding menu of a great restaurant – just look at that colour! Yet it's incredibly simple to make at home using familiar ingredients that I imagine you'll mostly already have to hand. You can definitely use frozen blackcurrants when fresh ones are out of season.

Serves 2
Takes 20 minutes

50g blackcurrants, stalks removed
tiny pinch sea salt flakes
1 tbsp lemon juice, plus a few zestings
3 tbsp caster sugar
100ml double cream
40g strained yoghurt

Place the blackcurrants, salt, lemon juice, zest and sugar in a small pan. Heat on high for 2–3 minutes until the blackcurrants have burst and you have a loose, bubbly jam. Pour onto a plate to quickly cool.

Meanwhile, gently whip the cream until soft peaks form (I just do this by hand, but you can use an electric mixer if you like). Fold in the yoghurt.

Once cool, stir in the jam then serve up, or pop in the fridge for up to a day ahead.

Originally published and printed in August 2024 by

Elliott's
21 Sciennes Road
Edinburgh
EH9 1NX

Second print-run, November 2024

elliottsedinburgh.com
@jess_elliott_dennison

All rights reserved. No part of this publication may be reproduced, stored in a retrieval system, or transmitted in any form by any means, electronic, mechanical, photocopying, recording or otherwise, without the prior written permission of the publishers and copyright owners.

Copyright text and photography © Jess Elliott Dennison

Design
Maeve Redmond

Illustration
Lilly Hedley

Food and Photography Assistant
Phoebe Moon

Copy Editing and Proofreading
Gemma Hinstridge

Printing
Gomer Press

ISBN 978-1-0686911-0-2
Printed in the UK

Created by food writer Jess Elliott Dennison, Elliott's celebrates simple cooking and life in the kitchen.

Elliott's Studio; a green-fronted tenement building on Sciennes Road in Edinburgh is an extension of Jess's home and where she cooks, writes recipes and teaches.

Jess's work is inspired by the produce, colours, textures and rituals that each season brings.

Find out more about all things Elliott's at
elliottsedinburgh.com
@jess_elliott_dennison